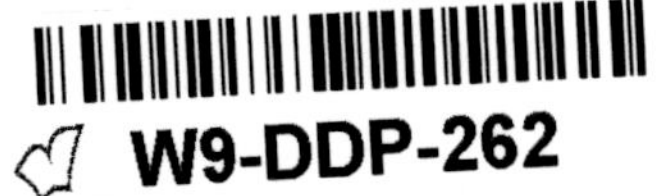

Pronunciation games

Mark Hancock

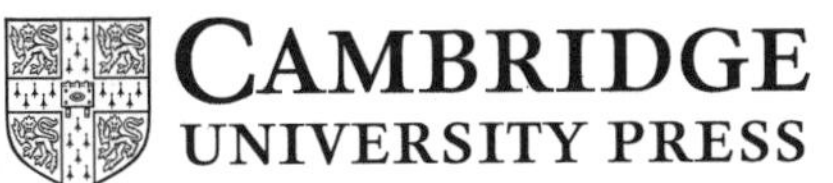

PUBLISHED BY THE PRESS SYNDICATE OF THE UNIVERSITY OF CAMBRIDGE
The Pitt Building, Trumpington Street, Cambridge, United Kingdom

CAMBRIDGE UNIVERSITY PRESS
The Edinburgh Building, Cambridge CB2 2RU, UK
40 West 20th Street, New York, NY 10011–4211, USA
477 Williamstown Road, Port Melbourne, VIC 3207, Australia
Ruiz de Alarcón 13, 28014 Madrid, Spain
Dock House, The Waterfront, Cape Town 8001, South Africa

http://www.cambridge.org

First published 1995
Twelfth printing 2004

Printed in the United Kingdom at the University Press, Cambridge

ISBN 0 521 46735 7 Resource book

Contents

Contents

Introduction

Pronunciation Games is a resource book for teachers containing photocopiable materials for use in the classroom. Each unit consists of a game designed to raise learners' awareness of an aspect of English pronunciation. The various activities are suitable for a wide range of levels and cover pronunciation points ranging from individual sounds and word stress to sentence stress and intonation.

Pronunciation is often taught through the teacher providing a model for learners to listen to and repeat. This is a valuable way of teaching pronunciation, but it neglects a need many learners feel to understand what they are doing. The activities in this book are intended to lead learners towards insights that will help them in their future learning career and reduce their dependence on the teacher as a model.

The pronunciation points in the book are presented in the form of games. There are a great variety of activities, from competitive games to problem-solving puzzles, from activities involving learners working individually to group and whole-class activities. What the games have in common, though, is that they engage learners in a challenge and, at the same time, highlight an aspect of pronunciation.

For convenience, the phonetic transcriptions of words provided in this book are as given in British-published dictionaries. These represent the accent called Received Pronunciation or RP. There is no implication that other accents are in any way wrong. Phonetic transcriptions are shown using the International Phonetic Alphabet (IPA). Where this is used, example words containing the sound are given so that the activity can be used whether or not learners know the IPA.

How to use this book

Point: 1 the pronunciation point covered by the game
Minimum level: 2 the minimum level of English required to play the game
Game type: 3 the type of game it is
Approximate time: 4 the approximate time the game takes

Rules

For most games the rules are given in both the teacher's notes and on the accompanying game page(s). The rules can be copied and given out to the class with the game.

The information above is provided just below the title of each game:

1 For an explanation of phonological terms that appear in the pronunciation point, refer to **Glossary of phonological terms** on pages 4-6.

2 The level given should be regarded as minimum; in other words, if the level indicated is elementary, the game may equally well be used at intermediate or advanced level if the class is unfamiliar with the pronunciation point.

3 For an explanation of the different types of games, refer to the section entitled **Game types and associated vocabulary** on page 7. Here, archetypes of the various games are briefly described, along with some of the particular vocabulary that a participant would need to play the game in English.

4 The time given is approximate in that it depends a lot on the class. Also, it is noticeable that as students play more pronunciation games, they tend to catch on much more quickly to the way the game works so that explanation time is significantly reduced.

The information provided for each game is divided into sections:

Preparation

This section explains the preparations that you will need to make before the lesson. In many cases this involves photocopying the game. Explanations of games, or checking answers at the end, can be made easier if you can also make a copy onto an OHP transparency or A3 size paper so that the whole class can see. It is also an advantage if you can copy boards or cards onto cardboard so that they can be re-used more often.

Presentation

For many games there is a section which suggests how to present the pronunciation point before the game.

Conducting the game

Guidelines are given for conducting the game.

Key

Keys are provided where appropriate.

Follow-up

In some instances suggestions for follow-up work or making other versions of the game are also provided.

Key

Key to phonetic symbols

Consonants

/p/	park, soap	/b/	be, rob		
/f/	face, laugh	/v/	very, save		
/t/	time, write	/d/	dog, road		
/θ/	thing, health	/ð/	these, breathe		
/tʃ/	church, question	/dʒ/	juice, page		
/s/	see, rice	/z/	zoo, rise		
/ʃ/	shoe, action	/ʒ/	vision, usual		
/k/	cat, black	/g/	go, bag		
/m/	make, same	/n/	name, rain	/ŋ/	sing, think
/h/	here, behind	/l/	live, feel	/r/	ride, arrive
/w/	went, away	/j/	yellow, use		

Vowels

/ə/	arrive, doctor, picture, Saturday, seven				
/æ/	cat, apple	/ʌ/	cut, up	/a:/	half, arm
/e/	men, any	/ɪ/	sit, in	/i:/	seat, me
/ɒ/	got, on	/ɔ:/	sport, war	/ɜ:/	girl, early
/ʊ/	should, good	/u:/	food, you		
/ɪə/	near, beer	/ʊə/	sure, tour	/eə/	air, area
/eɪ/	face, rain	/ɔɪ/	oil, boy	/aɪ/	line, eye
/əʊ/	go, over	/aʊ/	out, cow		

Glossary

Glossary of phonological terms

Assimilation

Assimilation is when a **phoneme** in a word is altered by the phoneme next to it. This can happen whether this neighbouring phoneme is in the same word or in a separate word. For example, in the phrase *did carefully* the second /d/ in *did* may actually be pronounced as /g/. Consequently, the phrase would sound like *dig carefully* /dɪgˈkeəfəlɪ/.

Consonant

Consonants are sounds made by blocking the flow of air coming out from the lungs. Sounds produced without this blockage are **vowels**. In the case of the sounds /j/ (as in *yellow*) and /w/ (as in *west*) the distinction is not very clear. These are called **semi-vowels**. The blockage of air may be accompanied by vibration of the vocal chords, in which case the consonant is **voiced**; if there is no vibration of the vocal chords, the consonant is **unvoiced**.

Consonant cluster

A consonant cluster is two or more consonant sounds together, for example, the /spr/ at the beginning of the word *spring* /sprɪŋ/. There are many combinations of consonants that are not possible, such as /ptf/. These combinations are different in different languages.

Contrastive stress

Contrastive stress is where we give emphasis to a word to contrast it with a word which has gone before. This happens for example when we correct someone, as in this exchange:

A My mother's name is John.
B You mean your father's name is John!

Diphthong

A diphthong is a complex **vowel**. It starts sounding like one vowel sound and then changes and ends sounding like another. An example is the vowel sound in *rain* /rein/.

Inflections

The past tense inflection *ed* is pronounced in three different ways, depending on the last sound in the verb. If the main verb ends with the sounds /t/ or /d/, *ed* is pronounced /ɪd/. If the verb ends with a **voiceless** consonant other than /t/, *ed* is pronounced /t/. If the verb ends with any other sound, *ed* is pronounced /d/. Examples of these three inflections are:

1 wanted = /ˈwɒntɪd/ **2** walked = /wɔ:kt/ **3** called = /kɔ:ld/

From the learner's point of view, the most important thing is that in 1 a syllable is added whereas in 2 and 3 no syllable is added.

The case is similar with the inflection *s* or *es* for plural forms, possessives or verbs in the present simple tense. If a verb, for example, ends with one of these sounds /s/, /z/, /ʃ/, /ʒ/, /tʃ/ or /dʒ/, the *s* is pronounced /ɪz/. If it ends with a voiceless consonant, the *s* is pronounced /s/. If the verb ends with any other sound, the *s* is pronounced /z/. Examples are:

1 washes = /ˈwɒʃɪz/ **2** drinks = /drɪnks/ **3** drives = /draɪvz/

Again, a syllable is added in 1 but not in 2 or 3.

Intonation

Intonation is the pattern of **prominence** and **tone** in speech. These can be compared to rhythm and melody in music. Intonation is used to convey extra meaning in speech beyond the meaning of the words. For example, intonation can be used to make *How nice!* sound enthusiastic or sarcastic.

Intrusive *r*

The intrusive *r* is an /r/ sound introduced between words where the first word ends with a vowel sound and the second word begins with a vowel sound. The intrusive *r* is not evident in the spelling of the words. For example, *law and order* may be pronounced /ˈlɔ:rənˈɔ:də/; the /r/ sound in the middle is an intrusive *r*.

Glossary

Linking sounds

A linking sound is a sound introduced between words where the first word ends with a vowel sound and the second word begins with a vowel sound. The linking sounds may be /j/ (as in _yellow_), /w/ (as in _wet_) or /r/ (as in _red_). Which of these sounds is inserted depends on the vowel that comes before it. Examples are:

me and you /ˈmiːjənˈyuː/
go and see /ˈgəʊwənˈsiː/
far and wide /ˈfaːrənˈwaid/ (Note in RP, *far* on its own is pronounced /faː/.)

If an /r/ is introduced where it is not evident in the spelling, this is then called an **intrusive r**. Some speakers regard this as incorrect pronunciation.

Minimal pair

A minimal pair is a pair of words that differ only in one **sound**, for example *flight* and *fright* or *cut* and *cat*. If the speaker fails to pronounce that one sound distinctly in one of the words, the listener could in theory think that the speaker had said the other word. For example, if a speaker fails to distinguish the sounds /r/ and /l/ in saying *I had a terrible flight*, he or she may be understood to have said *I had a terrible fright*. In practice, the context usually makes it obvious which word was meant. However, minimal pairs are useful in teaching because they focus attention clearly on individual sounds.

Phoneme

A phoneme is a sound which is significant in a language. For example, in a **minimal pair**, the two words differ only in one phoneme. Different languages have different phonemes. For example, Portuguese does not contain the phonemes /ɪ/ (as in *fit* /fɪt/) or /iː/ (as in *feet* /fɪːt/). Instead, it has a phoneme somewhere between the two. This may cause difficulty when the Portuguese learner of English tries to distinguish these phonemes. Another word for phoneme is **sound**.

Phonetic script

A phonetic script is an alphabet in which there is one symbol to represent each **phoneme** in a language. The normal English alphabet is largely conventional, that is, words are spelt according to agreed convention rather than according to sound. A phonetic script is then needed to show how words are pronounced. It is a useful language learning tool because it enables the learner to analyse pronunciation more clearly and refer to the dictionary for pronunciation.

Prominence

Prominence is emphasis given to particular words in speech to highlight them as important. For example, in **contrastive stress**, prominence is given to a word which contrasts with one that went before.

Received pronunciation

This is a standard British English accent which shows no regional variation. It is sometimes called British English.

Rhythm

Rhythm is the way a language sounds as a result of the pattern of stressed and unstressed syllables in speech. Rhythms are different between languages and contribute to the characteristic sound different languages have. A distinction can be made here between **stress-timed** languages and **syllable-timed** languages.

Sound

A sound is a **phoneme**. In teaching pronunciation, it is often necessary to make it clear when you are talking about sounds and when you are talking about letters. For example, *MP (Member of Parliament)* begins with a consonant if we are talking about written letters, but if we pronounce it, it begins with a vowel sound /empiː/.

Stress

Stress is emphasis given to **syllables** in words. For example, in the word *television* /teləˈvɪʒen/, the stress is on the third syllable. Often, words that look very similar in two languages actually have the stress in a different place, making them sound quite different. It is useful in teaching about stress to use symbols to represent stress patterns. For example, *television* could be represented as ••●•. Here, each circle represents a syllable and the bigger circle represents the stressed syllable. These symbols are used in this book. The stress patterns of words can change in the context of speech under the influence of surrounding words. For example, the stress on *teen* in *fourteen* /fɔːˈtiːn/ may be lost in the phrase *fourteen days*. This is called **stress shift**.

Stress may also move in words when suffixes are added. For example, look at the changed position of the stressed syllable (underlined) in these two words; _photograph, photography._ Changing the position of the stressed syllable in a word can change its meaning in some cases. For example, _export_ (with the stress on the first syllable) is a noun while _export_ (with the stress on the second syllable) is a verb.

Glossary

Stress-timed

A stress-timed language such as English has the stressed syllables in speech at more or less equal intervals. This happens however many unstressed syllables occur between the stressed syllables - if there are a lot of syllables, they have to be compressed. For example, these two phrases should take about the same time to say since each has three stressed syllables (underlined): *<u>Ring</u> <u>Jack</u> <u>soon</u>, <u>Tel</u>ephone <u>Al</u>ison <u>af</u>terwards.*

Syllable

A syllable is one vowel sound and any consonant sounds that are pronounced with it in a word. The vowel is the essential element except in the case of **syllabic consonants**. These are consonants that may form a syllable on their own, for example the /n/ sound in the word *cotton* /kɒtn/. The importance of the vowel in forming a syllable can be seen in the following example; *want* /wɒnt/ and *help* /help/ are both words of one syllable. In the past tense *wanted* /wɒntɪd/ has two syllables but *helped* /helpt/ still has only one. In the first case, both a vowel and a consonant are added, but in the second, only a consonant is added.

We must distinguish the idea of a syllable in pronunciation from the idea of a syllable in writing. The written syllable is a grouping of letters which may not be split between lines when a word is split, but in pronunciation the syllable is defined by sounds rather than letters.

Syllable-timed

A syllable-timed language such as French gives more or less equal emphasis to each of the syllables in speech, in contrast to a **stress-timed** language such as English.

Tone

Tone is the melody of speech, that is the rising and falling in pitch. Tone adds an extra level of meaning to what is said. For example, the tag question in *Madras is in India, isn't it?* may have a rising or a falling tone. A rising tone makes it sound as if the speaker is not very sure that Madras is in India, so that it is a genuine question. A falling tone makes it sound as if the speaker is fairly sure that Madras is in India and merely wants confirmation.

Tone unit

A tone unit is a section of speech containing one distinct pitch movement or **tone**. Within the tone unit, one word is emphasised by the speaker, and the stressed syllable in this word is the **tonic syllable** in the tone unit. The pitch movement, or tone, begins on this tonic syllable and continues to the end of the tone unit.

Tonic syllable

The tonic syllable is the stressed syllable in the word a speaker has chosen to emphasise. The speaker may choose to emphasise a word to indicate its importance. Consider this exchange:

A How long have you lived here?

B About two years. How long have <u>you</u> lived here?

Here, B emphasises *you* to signal a change in the subject of the conversation from B's personal history to A's personal history.

Vowel

A vowel is a sound produced when the flow of air from the lungs is not blocked and the vocal chords are vibrating. Different vowels can be produced by changing the position of the tongue. Which vowel is produced depends on which part of the tongue is raised and how far it is raised. A sound which starts as one vowel sound and ends as another is called a **diphthong**. Vowels can vary in length and in the IPA phonetic script the longer vowels have two dots or small triangles after them.

Weak form

A weak form is the way one of a number of common words in English is pronounced where it is not being emphasised for some reason. For example, the word *her* in *What's her name?* /ˈwɒts (h)ə ˈneɪm/ will be pronounced with a short vowel sound and possibly without the /h/ sound. But, in *It's <u>her</u> that I saw,* /ɪts ˈhɜː ðət aɪ sɔː/, *her* is emphasised and so the vowel sound is longer and the /h/ is pronounced.

Words which tend to have weak forms are grammatical words such as pronouns, eg, *her, him,* auxiliary verbs, eg, *can, are, does, has, was,* prepositions, eg, *to, at, for, from* and connectives, eg, *but, and.*

The short vowel sound in weak forms is always the **weak vowel** /ə/, except when the original vowel was /ɪ/, in which case it stays the same.

Game types

Game types and associated vocabulary

Battleships

Battleships is a guessing game for two players. Each player has a map of an area of sea with a grid of coordinates formed by, for example, letters across the top of the map and numbers down the side. Players draw ships on the map. They then must guess where the other player has placed his or her ships. To do this, players take turns to name one of the squares in the grid; their partner must say if a ship or part of a ship is in that square by saying *hit* or *miss*. The winner is the first player to find all the other player's ships.

Bingo

Bingo is a listen and find game for a large number of players. Each player has a grid on which are written different numbers. The person conducting the game calls out numbers. Players must look for and cross out the numbers as they are called out on the grid they have in front of them. A player can win at any point during the game by calling out *Bingo!* when they have crossed out every number in a line in the grid, but the final winner is the first player to cross out every number in the grid.

Happy Families

Happy families is a collecting game for a small number of players. One of the players shuffles the pack of cards and deals cards to each player. On the cards are pictures of members of families with their names below; each family has four members. The object of the game is for players to collect families. To do this, they take turns to ask other players for particular cards, and if the player asked has the card, he or she must give it to the person who asked for it. The player who has collected the most families at the end of the game is the winner.

Ludo

Ludo is a racing game. A small number of players sit around a board on which there is a path of squares from a start to a finish. Players place their counters on the start and take turns to throw the dice and move according to the number they have thrown. They then race along the path and the first player to reach the finish is the winner.

Mazes

A maze is a path-finding puzzle for one player. It consists of a map of a system of pathways with only one entrance and exit. The object is to find a route between these.

Noughts and crosses

Noughts and crosses is a blocking game for two players. Each player draws a square grid of nine squares. One player has the symbol X and the other player has the symbol O. The players take turns to draw their symbol in the squares. The winner is the first player to form a line of three squares in either a horizontal, vertical or diagonal direction. One of the main strategies in the game is to try to block the other player by occupying a square which he or she needs to form a line.

Snap

Snap is a matching game for two players. One of the players shuffles the pack of cards and deals cards to each player. Players then take turns to place cards face up in a pile on the table. If the design on one card is the same as on the card which has just been played, the first player to notice that the cards are the same can win all the cards on the table by calling *Snap!* When players no longer have any cards in their hands, one player shuffles and deals the cards from the pile again. The player with most cards when all the cards have been paired off is the winner.

Spot the differences

Spot the differences is a look and find puzzle. Players must spot differences between two almost identical pictures.

Making tracks

A

Point: counting syllables
Minimum level: elementary
Game type: a dice and board blocking game for two players
Approximate time: 20 minutes

Rules

1 Play this game in pairs. To win the game, you must get more points than the other player.

2 To win points, you must make a 'track'. A track is a straight line of four or more squares. The track can be horizontal ➡, vertical ⬇ or diagonal ⬊.

3 To make a track, you must win squares which are next to each other. You can win a square by throwing the dice. If the dice shows 1 or 4, you can win any square with a one-syllable word in it. If the dice shows 2 or 5, you can win any square with a two-syllable word in it. If the dice shows 3 or 6, you can win any square with a three-syllable word in it.

⚀ 1 syllable ⚃ 1 syllable
⚁ 2 syllables ⚄ 2 syllables
⚂ 3 syllables ⚅ 3 syllables

4 Players take turns to throw the dice and win squares. When you win a square, draw your symbol in it. One player can use the symbol X and the other player can use the symbol O.

5 When all the squares are full, count your points; four points for every track of four squares, five points for every track of five squares and six points for every track of six squares.

Preparation

Make a copy of the board and provide a dice for each pair of students in the class.

Presentation

1 Write the following words on the board:

train blouse eight coat

Point out that although these words all contain more than one written vowel, they only contain one vowel sound. They are therefore one-syllable words.

2 Write the following words on the board:

sunny about later started

Elicit that these words all contain two vowel sounds and therefore two syllables.

3 Write some three-syllable words from your course on the board. Elicit that these words all contain three vowel sounds and therefore three syllables. Then rub out all the words from the board. Call out the words in random order. Ask students to identify how many syllables each word contains.

4 Write a few words from the game on the board. Ask students to say how many syllables each word contains.

Conducting the game

1 Divide the class into pairs and give each pair a board and a dice.

2 Explain and/or give out the rules.

3 When students have finished, quickly read out the words in the grid and ask students to say how many syllables each word has.

Key

one syllable - car, cheese, jeans, bird, night, mouth, green, fruit, shoes, eight, school, blouse, train

two syllables - sunny, trousers, little, yellow, airport, tennis, bottles, morning, football, number, something

three syllables - bicycle, understand, aeroplane, newspaper, telephone, elephant, cinema, photograph, remember, banana, beautiful, somebody

Making your own versions

You can make your own boards for this game using vocabulary from your course.

Rules

1 Play this game in pairs. To win the game, you must get more points than the other player.

2 To win points, you must make a 'track'. A track is a straight line of four or more squares. The track can be horizontal ➡, vertical ⬇ or diagonal ⬊.

3 To make a track, you must win squares which are next to each other. You can win a square by throwing the dice. If the dice shows 1 or 4, you can win any square with a one-syllable word in it. If the dice shows 2 or 5, you can win any square with a two-syllable word in it. If the dice shows 3 or 6, you can win any square with a three-syllable word in it.

Dice		Dice	
⚀	1 syllable	⚃	1 syllable
⚁	2 syllables	⚄	2 syllables
⚂	3 syllables	⚅	3 syllables

4 Players take turns to throw the dice and win squares. When you win a square, draw your symbol in it. One player can use the symbol X and the other player can use the symbol O.

5 When all the squares are full, count your points; four points for every track of four squares, five points for every track of five squares and six points for every track of six squares.

car	bicycle	cheese	sunny	jeans	understand
bird	trousers	little	night	aeroplane	yellow
newspaper	mouth	airport	telephone	tennis	green
bottles	elephant	morning	fruit	cinema	football
shoes	photograph	eight	remember	school	blouse
banana	number	beautiful	train	somebody	something

Syllable soup

A

Point: syllables and stress in words with three or four syllables
Minimum level: intermediate
Game type: a look and find puzzle for students working individually (or in pairs)
Approximate time: 15 minutes

Preparation

Make a copy of the puzzle for each member of the class. You may also want to make a copy on an OHP transparency or a large piece of paper.

Presentation

1 Write a word with its syllables separated in random order on the board. For example, write *tomorrow* like this:

mor to row

2 Ask students to make the word out of these syllables.
3 Pronounce the word several times and ask students to identify the strongest or stressed syllable.
4 Write the word in the following grid to show the conventions used in the 'soup', that is, a circle around the first syllable and a square round the stressed syllable.

to	mor	row

Conducting the game

1 Give each student a puzzle. Explain that there are 14 words hidden in the grid. The words are horizontal ➡ or vertical ⬇. The stressed syllables have been removed from the words and placed outside the grid. All the first syllables are also outside the grid and begin with capital letters.
2 Demonstrate the activity by making two or three of the words in the puzzle. (Use your OHP transparency or large piece of paper if you have copied the puzzle.) The words, once they are discovered, should be circled and the syllables outside the grid should be crossed out.
3 If students have any difficulty getting started after this demonstration, give some or all of the words that they are looking for. They could also play the game in pairs.
4 When students have finished, check answers together. (Again, you can use your OHP transparency or large piece of paper.) Drill the pronunciation of the words.

Key

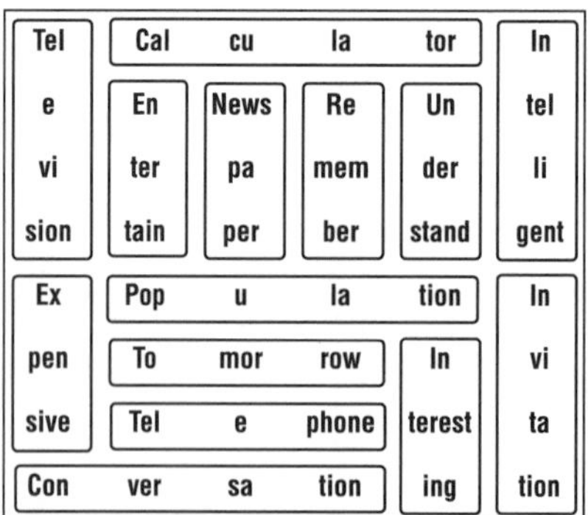

Tel	Cal	cu	la	tor	In
e	En	News	Re	Un	tel
vi	ter	pa	mem	der	li
sion	tain	per	ber	stand	gent
Ex	Pop	u	la	tion	In
pen	To	mor	row	In	vi
sive	Tel	e	phone	terest	ta
Con	ver	sa	tion	ing	tion

Making your own versions

1 Draw a grid. Fill the grid with words separated into syllables. Most dictionaries indicate how words are divided into syllables. The words may be written horizontally or vertically.
2 Put a circle around all first syllables and a square around all stressed syllables.
3 Finally, make a clean copy with the syllables in squares or circles removed from the grid and written outside it. Use an initial capital letter for the first syllable in each word.

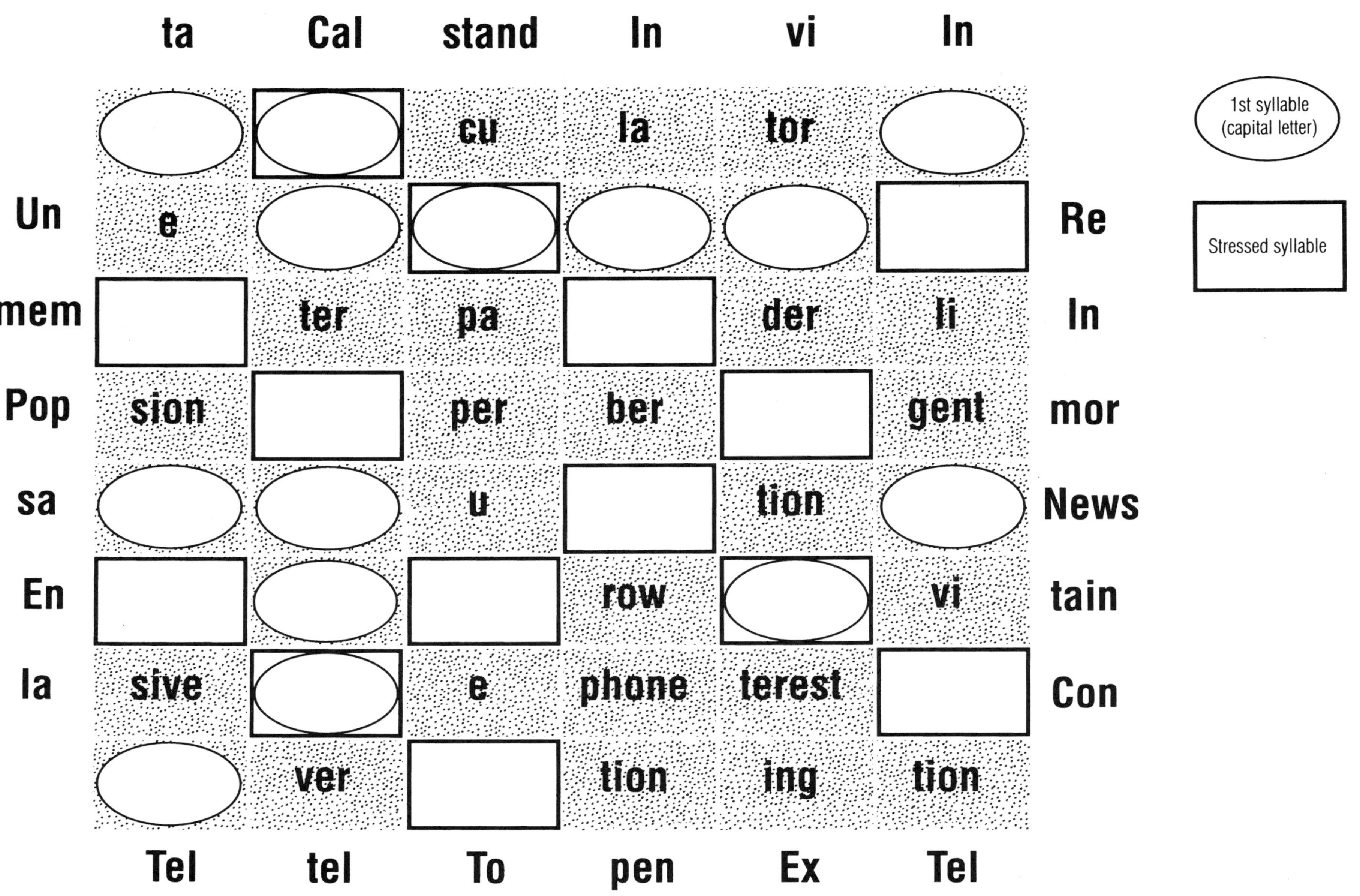
1st syllable (capital letter)
Stressed syllable
ta Cal stand In vi In
cu la tor
Un e Re
mem ter pa der li In
Pop sion per ber gent mor
sa u tion News
En row vi tain
la sive e phone terest Con
ver tion ing tion
Tel tel To pen Ex Tel

Cluster busters

A

Point: consonant clusters and syllables
Minimum level: intermediate
Game type: a blocking game for two teams
Approximate time: 30 minutes

Rules

1 To win this game, your team must make a complete line of squares so that you have a path from one side of the board to the other or from the top of the board to the bottom.

2 Team A must make a line from side to side and Team B must make a line from top to bottom like this, for example:

	A	A	A	A
A	A			

			B	
	B	B	B	
	B			
	B	B		
		B		

Diagonals like this are not accepted as a complete line:

		B
	B	
B		

3 To win a square, the team must say which square they want, eg *4C*, and add single consonant sounds to the word in the square to make another word. This must be done twice if the square has *2* written in it and three times if the square has *3* written in it.

4 Teams take turns to try to win squares.

5 You can try to stop the other team making a line by winning squares to block them. For example, here Team A blocks Team B's line:

		B		
		B		
		B		
		B		
		A		

Preparation

Copy the grid onto the board (or an OHP transparency). Make a copy of the grid for each student if students are going to play the game in smaller groups. Make a copy of the answer key for each group of students.

Presentation

1 Write the following sequence of words on the board:

or - ought - port - sport - sports

Point out that the vowel sound in these words remains the same even though the spelling is changed. Show that the words are built up by successively adding one consonant sound and that they all contain only one vowel sound and therefore one syllable. Stress that it is consonant sounds and not written consonants that are added. Thus, *he* cannot be expanded to *she* by adding an *s*; in this case, the consonant sound is changed, as opposed to a consonant sound being added.

2 Invite students to build up other words by adding single consonant sounds to *or*, such as:

or - law - floor - floors

or - four -force - forced

3 Ask students in groups to build up words from *eye*, such as:

eye - lie - light - flight - flights

eye - lie - like - liked

(Note that while no additional vowel sound (and therefore syllable) is added in the past tense ending in *liked*, this is not always the case, eg *wanted*. Adding an extra syllable as in this case is not acceptable in the game. Nor is it acceptable in plural endings, eg *prizes*, or third person singular verb endings, eg *watches*, which produce an additional syllable.)

Conducting the game

1 The game can be played as a class or with the class divided into several groups. The class or groups should be divided into two teams. If playing in groups, one student should be nominated as judge and given an answer key. If playing as a class, the teacher can be the judge.

2 Explain that all the words in the grid can be expanded by adding single consonant sounds. All the words can be expanded in this way twice and some can be expanded three times.

3 Explain and/or give out the rules. Note that an alternative way of winning the game would be for a team to win four squares in a row rather than make a complete line of squares from one side of the board to the other.

4 As teams produce their sequences of words, the words should be written in pencil in the box with the original word. (The words can be rubbed out if they are incorrect.) The team can be asked to pronounce the sequence to demonstrate that all the words have only one syllable.

5 If the sequence offered is different from that in the key, the teacher can be consulted to see if the alternative is acceptable.

6 Write the letter of the team in the squares as they are won.

Cluster busters

Key

These are suggested answers but others are possible.

	A	B	C	D	E
1	LIME climb climbs	WHY white quite	ICE rice price	KEY ski skis	LOCK clock clocks
2	ILL fill filled	EIGHT late plate plates	ACHE take steak steaks	RAY pray spray sprays	WHOLE hold holds
3	WIN wind winds	OWE low slow slows	LAY late plate plates	TEA team steam steams	COOL school schools
4	NECK necks next	PAY pain paint paints	EYE eyes lies flies	ART tart start starts	ACE face faced
5	POT spot spots	EYES lies flies	HELL help helps	THING think thinks	IN pin spin

B

A

A3 Cluster busters

	A	B	C	D	E
1	LIME (2)	WHY (2)	ICE (2)	KEY (2)	LOCK (2)
2	ILL (2)	EIGHT (3)	ACHE (3)	RAY (3)	WHOLE (2)
3	WIN (2)	OWE (3)	LAY (3)	TEA (3)	COOL (2)
4	NECK (2)	PAY (3)	EYE (3)	ART (3)	ACE (2)
5	POT (2)	EYES (2)	HELL (2)	THING (2)	IN (2)

B

A

Rules

1 To win this game, your team must make a complete line of squares so that you have a path from one side of the board to the other or from the top of the board to the bottom.

2 Team A must make a line from side to side and Team B must make a line from top to bottom like this, for example:

	A	A	A	A
A	A			

			B	
	B	B	B	
	B			
	B	B		
		B		

Diagonals like this are not accepted as a complete line:

		B
	B	
B		

3 To win a square, the team must say which square they want, eg *4C*, and add single consonant sounds to the word in the square to make another word. This must be done twice if the square has *2* written in it and three times if the square has *3* written in it.

4 Teams take turns to try to win squares.

5 You can try to stop the other team making a line by winning squares to block them. For example, here Team A blocks Team B's line:

		B		
		B		
		B		
		B		
		A		

Stress moves

Point: patterns of word stress
Minimum level: elementary
Game type: a game of physical movement for the whole class
Approximate time: 20 minutes

Rules

1 One player begins the game by saying his or her own word with the appropriate stress move(s) and then saying another player's word with the appropriate stress move(s). This player then continues by saying his or her own word with the appropriate stress move(s) and then saying yet another player's word with the appropriate stress move(s). The game continues in this way until someone makes a mistake. A mistake occurs when a player:
- fails to respond when his or her word is called.
- forgets to repeat his or her own word first.
- pronounces a word incorrectly.
- makes the wrong stress move(s).

2 Each player begins with 10 points and loses one point for each mistake. After a mistake, the game must be restarted by the teacher or by the player who made the mistake.

3 Finish the game when one player has lost all 10 points. If students are still enthusiastic, ask them to swap their flashcards and begin the game again.

Preparation

1 Choose about 20 words from your course or ask each member of the class to suggest a word. Make sure that the words contain a number of different stress patterns. Here are some examples:

1 ●	**2 ●•**	**3 •●**	**4 •●•**	**5 ●••**
jeans	monkey	balloon	banana	bicycle
blouse	trousers	cassette	detective	cinema
eight	yellow	goodbye	computer	telephone
mouth	morning	hello	umbrella	photograph

Write your words on flashcards.

2 Decide on some 'stress moves' before the class and practise them a little. Stress moves are physical movements which you make as you say the word. There should be one move to accompany the stressed syllable and a different move for each of the rest of the syllables. Here are some suggestions:

a Make a fist for each unstressed syllable and open your fingers for the stressed syllable.
b Clap your hands for each unstressed syllable and bang the desk for the stressed syllable.

Presentation

1 Choose some of the words you have decided upon and write them on the board. Point to the words in turn and read them out. Use the appropriate stress moves from the system you have chosen.

2 As students catch on to the way the stress moves work, invite members of the class to say some words with the appropriate stress moves.

3 If possible, ask students to sit in a circle so that they can all see each other. Distribute a flashcard to each student and ask everyone to practise saying the word on their card with the stress moves to accompany it. Then ask each student in turn to complete the sentence *My word is ...* with the appropriate stress move(s).

Conducting the game

Explain the rules and proceed with the game. With very big classes, play a demonstration game and then let students play the game in smaller groups.

Making your own versions

Once the stress move idea has been introduced, it can of course be used whenever you want to show the stress pattern of a word. The game can be played as revision at regular intervals.

Stress snap

Point: stress patterns in simple nouns
Minimum level: pre-intermediate
Game type: a matching game with cards for two players
Approximate time: 25 minutes

Rules

1 The aim of the game is to win more cards than your partner(s).

2 Divide the cards equally between you. Keep the cards face down in a pile.

3 Take turns to turn the cards face up in a pile on the table, making sure that the player cannot see the card before the others.

4 If you notice that the stress pattern of the word on a card is the same as the word on the card before, you can win all the cards in the pile. To do this, put your hand on the pile quickly and say *Snap!*

5 After you have won the pile, put the cards to one side and begin again taking turns to put cards on the table. Shuffle and deal the cards on the table again when you no longer have any cards in your hands.

6 The player with the most cards when all the cards have been paired off is the winner.

7 If you cannot agree with your partner(s) about the stress patterns of words, ask the teacher.

Preparation

Copy and cut out a set of cards for each pair of students in the class.

Presentation

1 Write the following words with their stress patterns on the board:

1 ●	2 ●•	3 •●	4 ●••	5 •●•
right	question	mistake	salary	pollution

2 Ask students to suggest other words with the same stress patterns; write these words on the board under the appropriate stress pattern.

3 Read out some of the words from the game and ask students which stress pattern they correspond to.

Conducting the game

1 Divide the class into pairs and give each pair a pack of cards. (The game could also be played by students in groups of three if necessary.)

2 Explain and/or give out the rules.

Key

1 ●	2 ●•	3 •●	4 ●••	5 •●•
shirt	money	balloon	continent	potato
ball	problem	shampoo	cinema	disaster
head	student	police	Saturday	computer
eye	mother	career	paragraph	banana
shoe	music	cartoon	elephant	tomato
girl	garden	address	manager	tobacco
light	island	defence	recipe	umbrella
train	colour	guitar	vehicle	professor

Making your own versions

You could make other packs of cards to include vocabulary from your course. You need an even number of words for each stress pattern and about the same number of words for each of the stress patterns you decide to include.

shirt	ball	head	eye
shirt	ball	head	eye
shoe	girl	light	train
shoe	girl	light	train
money	problem	student	mother
money	problem	student	mother
music	garden	island	colour
music	garden	island	colour
balloon	shampoo	police	career
balloon	shampoo	police	career

Rules

1 The aim of the game is to win more cards than your partner(s).

2 Divide the cards equally between you. Keep the cards face down in a pile.

3 Take turns to turn the cards face up in a pile on the table, making sure that the player cannot see the card before the others.

4 If you notice that the stress pattern of the word on a card is the same as the word on the card before, you can win all the cards in the pile. To do this, put your hand on the pile quickly and say *Snap!*

5 After you have won the pile, put the cards to one side and begin again taking turns to put cards on the table. Shuffle and deal the cards on the table again when you no longer have any cards in your hands.

6 The player with the most cards when all the cards have been paired off is the winner.

7 If you cannot agree with your partner(s) about the stress patterns of words, ask the teacher.

A5 Stress snap Sheet 2

Rules

1 The aim of the game is to win more cards than your partner(s).

2 Divide the cards equally between you. Keep the cards face down in a pile.

3 Take turns to turn the cards face up in a pile on the table, making sure that the player cannot see the card before the others.

4 If you notice that the stress pattern of the word on a card is the same as the word on the card before, you can win all the cards in the pile. To do this, put your hand on the pile quickly and say *Snap!*

5 After you have won the pile, put the cards to one side and begin again taking turns to put cards on the table. Shuffle and deal the cards on the table again when you no longer have any cards in your hands.

6 The player with the most cards when all the cards have been paired off is the winner.

7 If you cannot agree with your partner(s) about the stress patterns of words, ask the teacher.

guitar / guitar	defence / defence	address / address	cartoon / cartoon
paragraph / paragraph	Saturday / Saturday	cinema / cinema	continent / continent
vehicle / vehicle	recipe / recipe	manager / manager	elephant / elephant
banana / banana	computer / computer	disaster / disaster	potato / potato
professor / professor	umbrella / umbrella	tobacco / tobacco	tomato / tomato

Stress dice

A

Point: stress patterns in adjectives
Minimum level: intermediate
Game type: a racing game with board and dice for three or four players
Approximate time: 30 minutes

Rules

1 Place your counters on the square marked *Start*. The object of the game is to move around the board from square to square to the square marked *Finish*. The first player to reach this square is the winner.

2 Players take turns to throw the dice and move.

3 Numbers on the dice correspond to stress patterns as follows:

To move, throw the dice and move to the first word you come to with the stress pattern indicated. (You can land on a square that already has a counter on it.)

4 If there is the tail of a worm in the square you have landed on, move your counter to its head.

5 If you land on a square marked *Miss a turn*, you miss your next turn.

6 If there are no more words with that stress pattern left before the finish, you can move to the finish.

Preparation

Make a copy of the board and provide a dice for each group of three or four students in the class. Provide a counter for each student.

Presentation

1 Write the following words with their stress patterns on the board:

1 ●	2 ●•	3 •●	4 ●••	5 •●•	6 ●•••
fat	happy	ashamed	innocent	important	supermarket

2 Ask students to think of other adjectives with the same stress patterns; write these words on the board under the appropriate stress pattern.

3 Read out some of the words from the game and ask students to say which stress pattern they correspond to.

Conducting the game

1 Divide the class into groups of three or four and give each group a board, a dice and counters.

2 Explain and/or give out the rules.

3 During the game, move around the class helping students to resolve any disputes.

4 When students have finished, drill the pronunciation of the words.

Key

1 ●	2 ●•	3 •●	4 ●••	5 •●•	6 ●•••
fair	easy	correct	difficult	disgusting	supermarket
tall	boring	alive	interesting	confusing	architecture
long	ugly	unfair	beautiful	unhappy	fortunately
strong	fatter	alone	popular	unfriendly	ceremony
short	cloudy	unknown	serious	informal	fascinating
		behind	sensitive	depressing	

Making your own versions

A blank version of the board is provided so that you can make your own version of the game using vocabulary from your course. You will need to make a list of five words each for three different stress patterns and six words each for three other stress patterns. Write these words on the board. Make sure that you distribute the words in random order so that the words with the same stress pattern are not all clustered together. Write a key with numbers 1-6 on the board to show which number on the dice corresponds to which stress pattern.

A6 Stress dice

Rules

1 Place your counters on the square marked *Start*. The object of the game is to move around the board from square to square to the square marked *Finish*. The first player to reach this square is the winner.

2 Players take turns to throw the dice and move.

3 Numbers on the dice correspond to stress patterns as follows:

Dice	Pattern	Dice	Pattern
1	●	4	●••
2	●•	5	•●•
3	•●	6	●•••

To move, throw the dice and move to the first word you come to with the stress pattern indicated. (You can land on a square that already has a counter on it.)

4 If there is the tail of a worm in the square you have landed on, move your counter to its head.

5 If you land on a square marked *Miss a turn*, you miss your next turn.

6 If there are no more words with that stress pattern left before the finish, you can move to the finish.

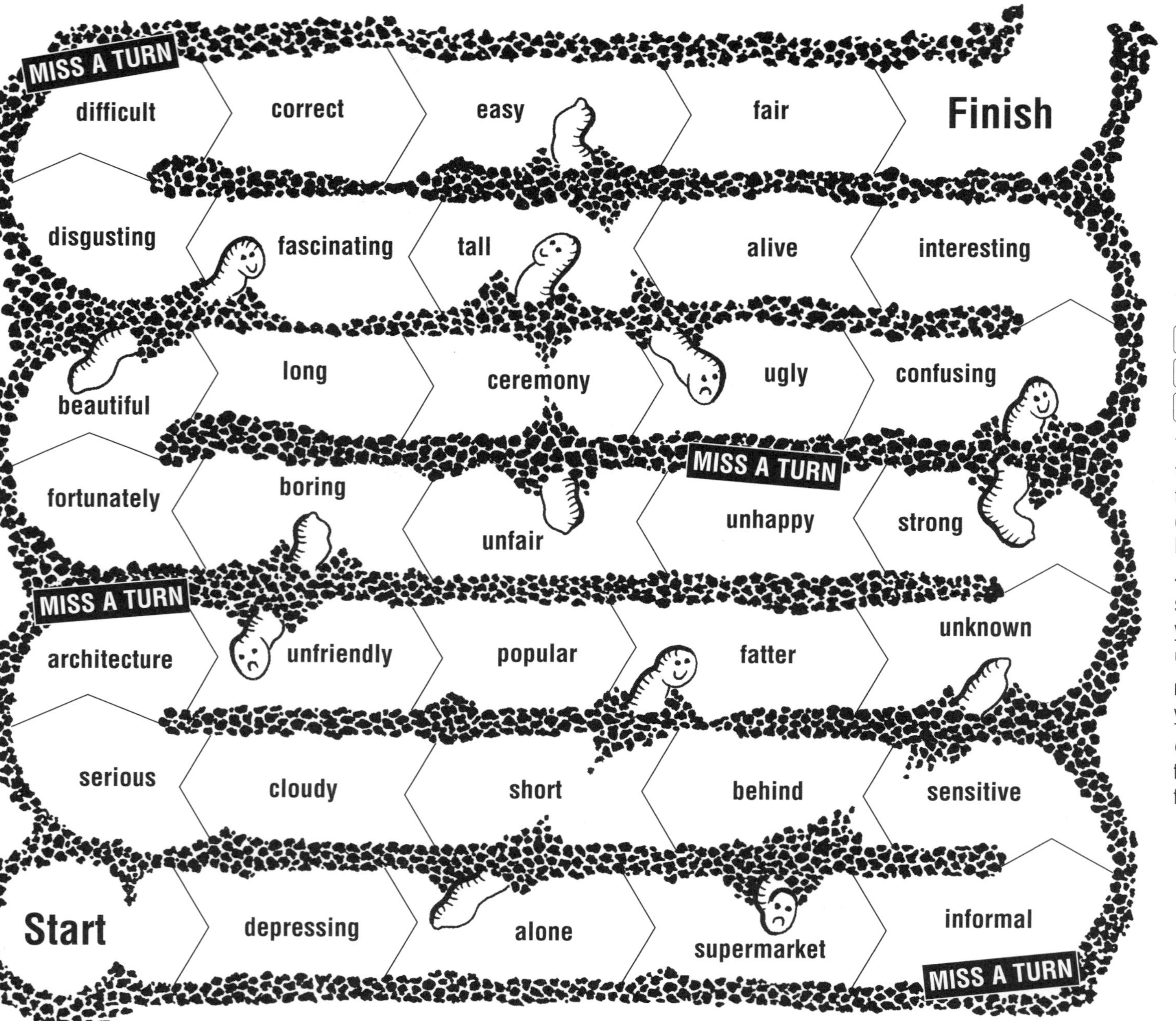

Finish

MISS A TURN

MISS A TURN

MISS A TURN

MISS A TURN

Start

Rules

1 Place your counters on the square marked *Start*. The object of the game is to move around the board from square to square to the square marked *Finish*. The first player to reach this square is the winner.

2 Players take turns to throw the dice and move.

3 Numbers on the dice correspond to stress patterns as follows:

To move, throw the dice and move to the first word you come to with the stress pattern indicated. (You can land on a square that already has a counter on it.)

4 If there is the tail of a worm in the square you have landed on, move your counter to its head.

5 If you land on a square marked *Miss a turn*, you miss your next turn.

6 If there are no more words with that stress pattern left before the finish, you can move to the finish.

Stepping stones

A

Point: stress in two-syllable verbs
Minimum level: pre-intermediate
Game type: a path-finding puzzle for students working individually (or in pairs)
Approximate time: 15 minutes

Preparation
Make a copy of the puzzle for each member of the class.

Presentation
Write the following verbs on the board:

borrow finish open
allow arrive relax

Elicit that the verbs in the first group have the stress on the first syllable and that the verbs in the second group have the stress on the second syllable. Point out that most two-syllable verbs have the stress on the second syllable.

Conducting the game
1 Give each student a puzzle. (The game could also be played in pairs.) Explain that the puzzle shows a river which must be crossed using the stepping stones. Point out that there is only one route across the river.
2 Explain that students may only use a stepping stone if the verb on it has the stress on the first syllable.
3 To cross the river, players are allowed to step from one stone to the next horizontally, vertically or diagonally. They may also step over a stone to the one beyond. The following diagram illustrates the moves that are allowed:

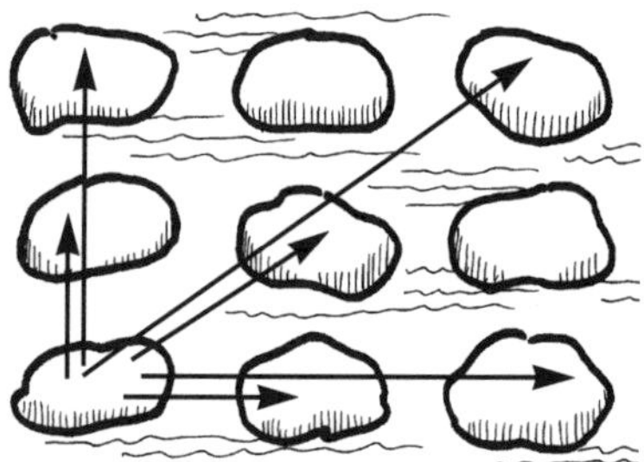

4 To reach the far bank of the river, players may also step over a stone.
5 When students have finished, check the route together. Point out that all the other verbs have the stress on the second syllable. Drill the pronunciation of the two groups of verbs.

Key
These are the stones you need to use to cross the river:

answer - cancel - copy - enter - happen - listen - manage - order - offer - suffer - wonder - worry

worry remove divide become forget

prefer invite behave attract respect

observe appear wonder explain suffer

repeat enjoy report support offer

collect manage advise order discuss

listen demand pronounce improve describe

happen deny repair supply decide

allow enter believe copy cancel

receive provide admit compare escape

correct regret answer belong invent

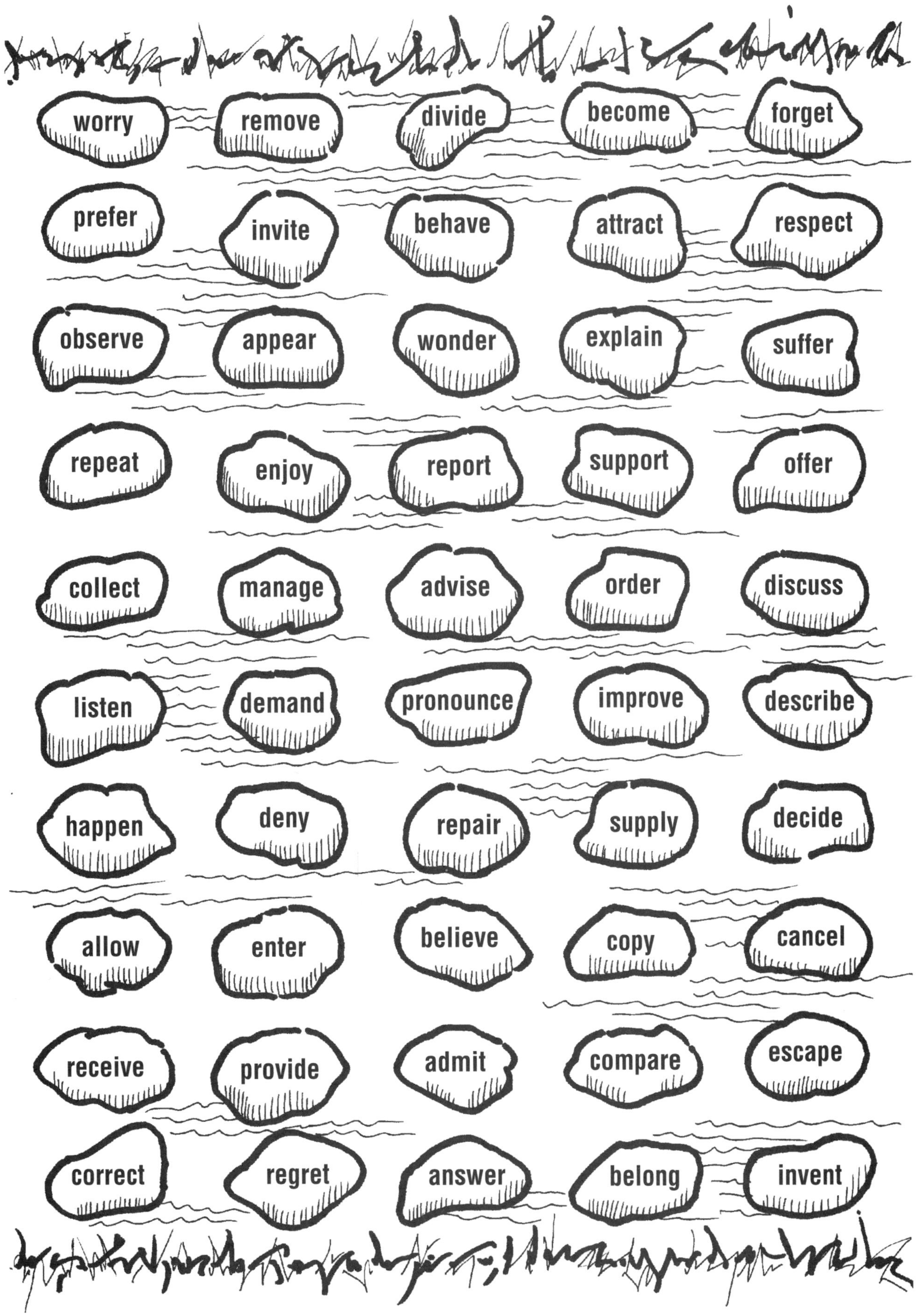

Chinese chequers

A

Point: when and when not to add a syllable in *ed* and *s/es* inflections
Minimum level: intermediate
Game type: a racing game with board and dice for three players
Approximate time: 40 minutes

Rules

1 Players each take a letter, A, B or C. They place their three counters on the three corresponding circles, at the bottom of the board.

2 The aim of the game is to move these three counters across the board to the three circles in the box opposite marked *home*. The first player to do this is the winner.

3 Players take turns to throw the dice and move. For each number on the dice there is a stress pattern indicated above and below the board. After throwing the dice, players can move one of their counters to a neighbouring hexagon if it contains the stress pattern indicated on the dice. If there isn't a neighbouring hexagon with the stress pattern indicated, players miss a turn.

4 Players may choose not to move if it is not to their advantage.

5 Only one counter can occupy a hexagon at a time.

6 Players can throw any number to enter the home box.

7 Players can jump straight across a hexagon occupied by another player's counter, like this:

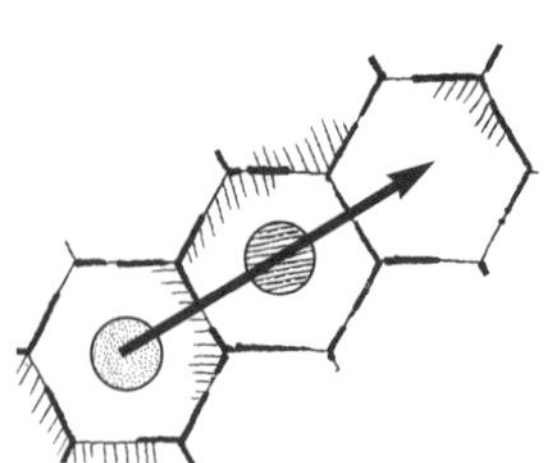

Preparation

Make a copy of the board and provide a dice for each group of three students in the class. Provide three counters for each student.

Presentation

Note that there is too much material here to cover in one lesson. You might like to use this game when the class is already familiar with the rule for the past tense inflection *ed*. The rule is that if a verb ends with the sounds /t/ or /d/, then a vowel sound, and therefore a syllable, is added to the past tense inflection. (See **Inflections** in the glossary for more information.)

1 Remind the class of the past tense inflection rule as stated above.

2 Explain that sometimes a syllable is added to words with *s* and *es* endings (as in plurals, 3rd person present simple verbs and possessives). Illustrate this point with these examples:

a apples	/ˈæpəlz/	**b** hates	/heɪts/	**c** Smith's	/smɪθs/
oranges	/ˈɒrɪndʒɪz/	watches	/ˈwɒtʃɪz/	Jones's	/ˈdʒəʊnzɪz/

For each pair of words, adding the *s* or *es* adds a syllable only in the second word.

3 Write these words on the board:

wash drive exercise scientist fax Alice John

Ask students to decide if a syllable is or is not added to these words.

4 Ask students to suggest the rule for the addition of syllables. An acceptable answer could be that you add a syllable if the last sound in the word is *s* or something similar. (The actual rule is that if the word ends with /s/, /z/, /ʃ/, /ʒ/, /tʃ/ or /dʒ/, another syllable is added. Note that the sound /ʒ/ is rare at the end of English words, so it may be best not to mention it in the rule.)

Conducting the game

1 Divide the class into groups of three students and give each group a board, a dice and counters. (The game could also be played by students in pairs if necessary.)

2 Explain and/or give out the rules.

3 During the game, move around the class helping students to resolve any disputes. You can also encourage them to look up stress patterns in the dictionary.

Key

1 ●	2 •●	3 ●•	4 •●•	5 ●••	6 ●•••
called	believed	answered	arranges	hospitals	ambulances
drives	depressed	frightened	completed	oranges	compensated
hates	describes	hated	delighted	scientists	estimated
Smith's	machines	needed	demanded	separates	exercises
talked	receives	wanted	invented	telephoned	Macintosh's
watched	returned	watches	relaxes	visited	realizes
					separated

Making your own versions

A blank version of the board is provided so that you can make your own version of the game using vocabulary from your course. You will need to make a list of six words for five stress patterns and seven words for one stress pattern. Write these words into the hexagons on the board. Make sure that you distribute the words in random order so that the words with the same stress pattern are not all clustered together.

Chinese chequers A8

Rules

1 Players each take a letter, A, B or C. They place their three counters on the three corresponding circles, at the bottom of the board.

2 The aim of the game is to move these three counters across the board to the three circles in the box opposite marked *home*. The first player to do this is the winner.

3 Players take turns to throw the dice and move. For each number on the dice there is a stress pattern indicated above and below the board. After throwing the dice, players can move one of their counters to a neighbouring hexagon if it contains the stress pattern indicated on the dice. If there isn't a neighbouring hexagon with the stress pattern indicated, players miss a turn.

4 Players may choose not to move if it is not to their advantage.

5 Only one counter can occupy a hexagon at a time.

6 Players can throw any number to enter the home box.

7 Players can jump straight across a hexagon occupied by another player's counter, like this:

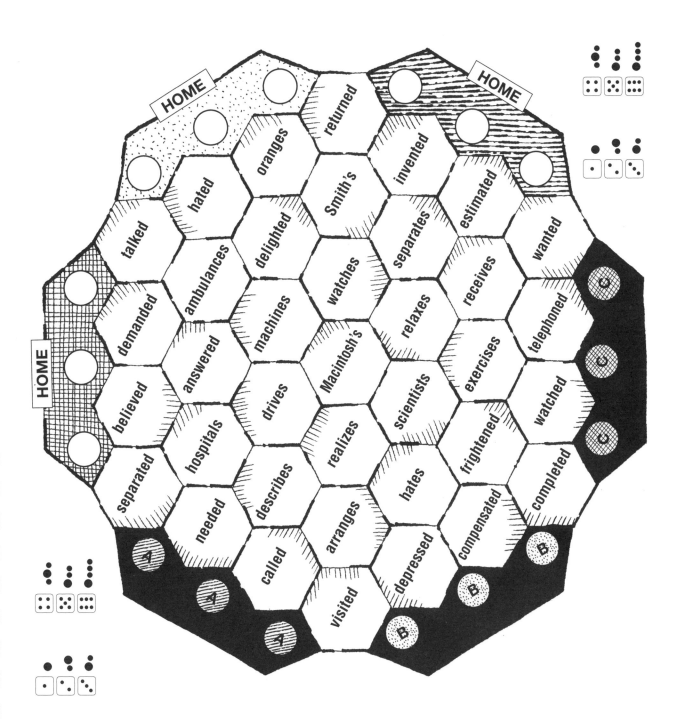

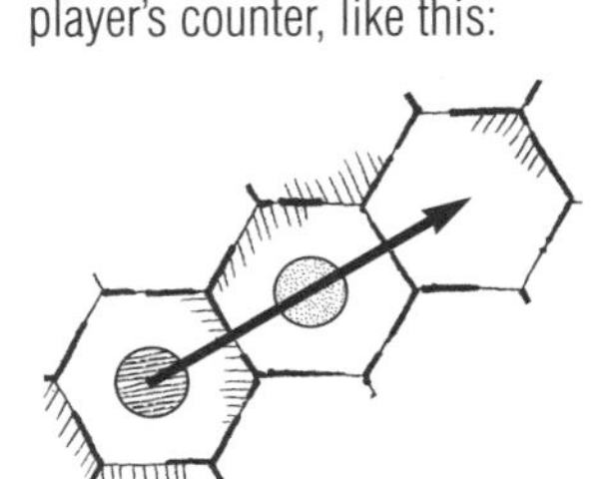

HOME

separated | believed | demanded | talked

needed | hospitals | answered | ambulances | hated

called | describes | drives | machines | delighted | oranges

visited | arranges | realizes | Macintosh's | watches | Smith's | returned

depressed | hates | scientists | relaxes | separates | invented

compensated | frightened | exercises | receives | estimated

completed | watched | telephoned | wanted

HOME

HOME

A A A

B B B

C C C

A8 Chinese chequers

Rules

1 Players each take a letter, A, B or C. They place their three counters on the three corresponding circles, at the bottom of the board.

2 The aim of the game is to move these three counters across the board to the three circles in the box opposite marked *home*. The first player to do this is the winner.

3 Players take turns to throw the dice and move. For each number on the dice there is a stress pattern indicated above and below the board. After throwing the dice, players can move one of their counters to a neighbouring hexagon if it contains the stress pattern indicated on the dice. If there isn't a neighbouring hexagon with the stress pattern indicated, players miss a turn.

4 Players may choose not to move if it is not to their advantage.

5 Only one counter can occupy a hexagon at a time.

6 Players can throw any number to enter the home box.

7 Players can jump straight across a hexagon occupied by another player's counter, like this:

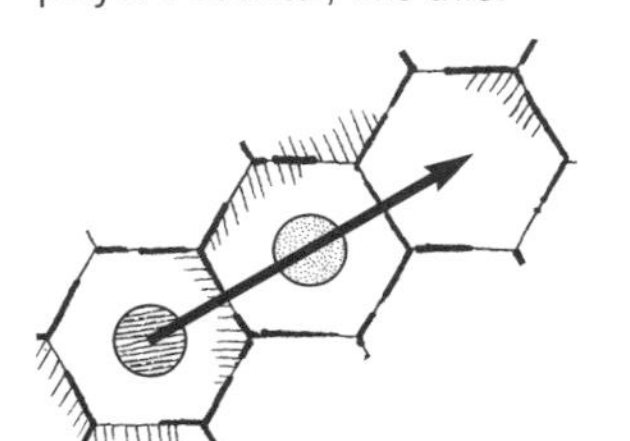

HOME

HOME

HOME

A A A

B B B

C C C

Happy Families

A

Point: stress patterns in long words
Minimum level: advanced
Game type: a collecting game with cards for four or five players
Approximate time: 50 minutes

Rules

1 The aim of the game is for each player to collect complete families of words such as: *civil - civility - civilize - civilization.*

2 The monitor deals out five cards to each player. Decide the order in which you are going to take turns.

3 Players take turns to request cards from any of the other players. For example: *Murat, can I have 'civility' please?* If the player that you ask has the word, they must give you it. You can then ask either this player or any other player for another card. If the player has not got the card, take another card from the monitor. It is now the next player's turn.

4 When you have a complete family, put the cards face down on the table.

5 The player with most families when all the families are complete, is the winner.

6 The job of the monitor is to make sure that players pronounce words correctly when they ask for them. If players do not pronounce words correctly, the monitor should ask them to repeat the word.

Preparation

Copy and cut out a set of cards for each group of four or five students in the class.

Presentation

These word families illustrate well the way certain suffixes affect the placement of word stress. The pattern is totally regular for all the families in this game.

1 Write these two word families on the board. Underline the stressed syllable in each word.
civil - civility - civilize - civilization
personal - personality - personalize - personalization

2 Draw attention to the stress patterns and their relationship with the suffixes. Then drill the pronunciation of the words in each family. You could also talk at this point about what parts of speech are formed by the addition of the suffixes. Note that, unlike the first words in the other families, *hospital* is a noun.

Conducting the game

1 Divide the class into groups of four or five. Nominate a monitor for each group.
2 Give each group a pack of cards and give each monitor a key.
3 Explain and/or give out the rules.

Key

civil	civility	civilize	civilization
equal	equality	equalize	equalization
fertile	fertility	fertilize	fertilization
final	finality	finalize	finalization
general	generality	generalize	generalization
hospital	hospitality	hospitalize	hospitalization
legal	legality	legalize	legalization
mobile	mobility	mobilize	mobilization
national	nationality	nationalize	nationalization
neutral	neutrality	neutralize	neutralization
personal	personality	personalize	personalization
real	reality	realize	realization
stable	stability	stabilize	stabilization
sterile	sterility	sterilize	sterilization

(Note that the first vowel is pronounced differently in *final* and *finality.* Note also that the letters *ea* represent one vowel sound in *real* but two vowel sounds in *reality.)*

A9 Happy Families Sheet 1

Rules

1 The aim of the game is for each player to collect complete families of words such as: *civil - civility - civilize - civilization.*

2 The monitor deals out five cards to each player. Decide the order in which you are going to take turns.

3 Players take turns to request cards from any of the other players. For example: *Murat, can I have 'civility' please?* If the player that you ask has the word, they must give you it. You can then ask either this player or any other player for another card. If the player has not got the card, take another card from the monitor. It is now the next player's turn.

4 When you have a complete family, put the cards face down on the table.

5 The player with most families when all the families are complete, is the winner.

6 The job of the monitor is to make sure that players pronounce words correctly when they ask for them. If players do not pronounce words correctly, the monitor should ask them to repeat the word.

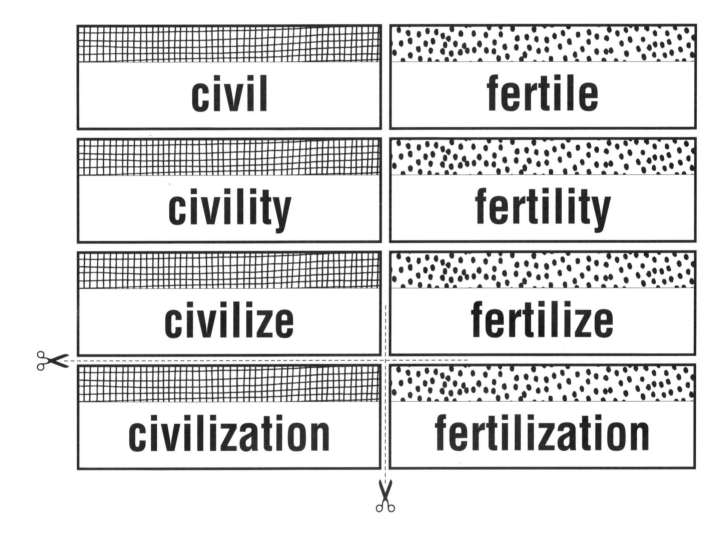

civil	**fertile**
civility	**fertility**
civilize	**fertilize**
civilization	**fertilization**

personal	final
personality	finality
personalize	finalize
personalization	finalization
national	stable
nationality	stability
nationalize	stabilize
nationalization	stabilization

A9 Happy Families Sheet 3

legal	neutral
legality	neutrality
legalize	neutralize
legalization	neutralization
mobile	real
mobility	reality
mobilize	realize
mobilization	realization

general	hospital
generality	hospitality
generalize	hospitalize
generalization	hospitalization
equal	sterile
equality	sterility
equalize	sterilize
equalization	sterilization

10 Stress maze

A

Point: word stress patterns
Minimum level: pre-intermediate
Game type: a path-finding puzzle for students working individually (or in pairs)
Approximate time: 15 minutes

Preparation

Make a copy of the maze for each member of the class.

Presentation

Write the following words on the board:

Germany grandmother restaurant
eleven policeman September

Elicit that all the words have three syllables. Then elicit that the words in the first group have the stress on the first syllable and that the words in the second group have the stress on the second syllable.

Conducting the game

1 Give each student a maze. (The game could also be played by students in pairs.)
2 Explain that the object of the game is to find a path from the entrance in the top left side of the maze to the exit in the bottom right.
3 Draw attention to the stress pattern ●•• below the maze and explain that you can only move across a square if it contains a word with this stress pattern.
4 You can move from one square to the next horizontally or vertically but not diagonally.
5 When students have finished, check the route together.

Key

The correct route is:

hamburger - Saturday - regular - possible - yesterday - passenger - holiday - traveller - telephone - recognise - officer - cinema - government - photograph - aeroplane - opposite - hospital

Making your own versions

If you want to make other versions of the puzzle to use vocabulary from your course, choose about 20 words with one particular stress pattern and write them on the grid so that they form a continuous path from entry to exit. Then fill the remaining squares with words with different stress patterns.

Stress maze A10

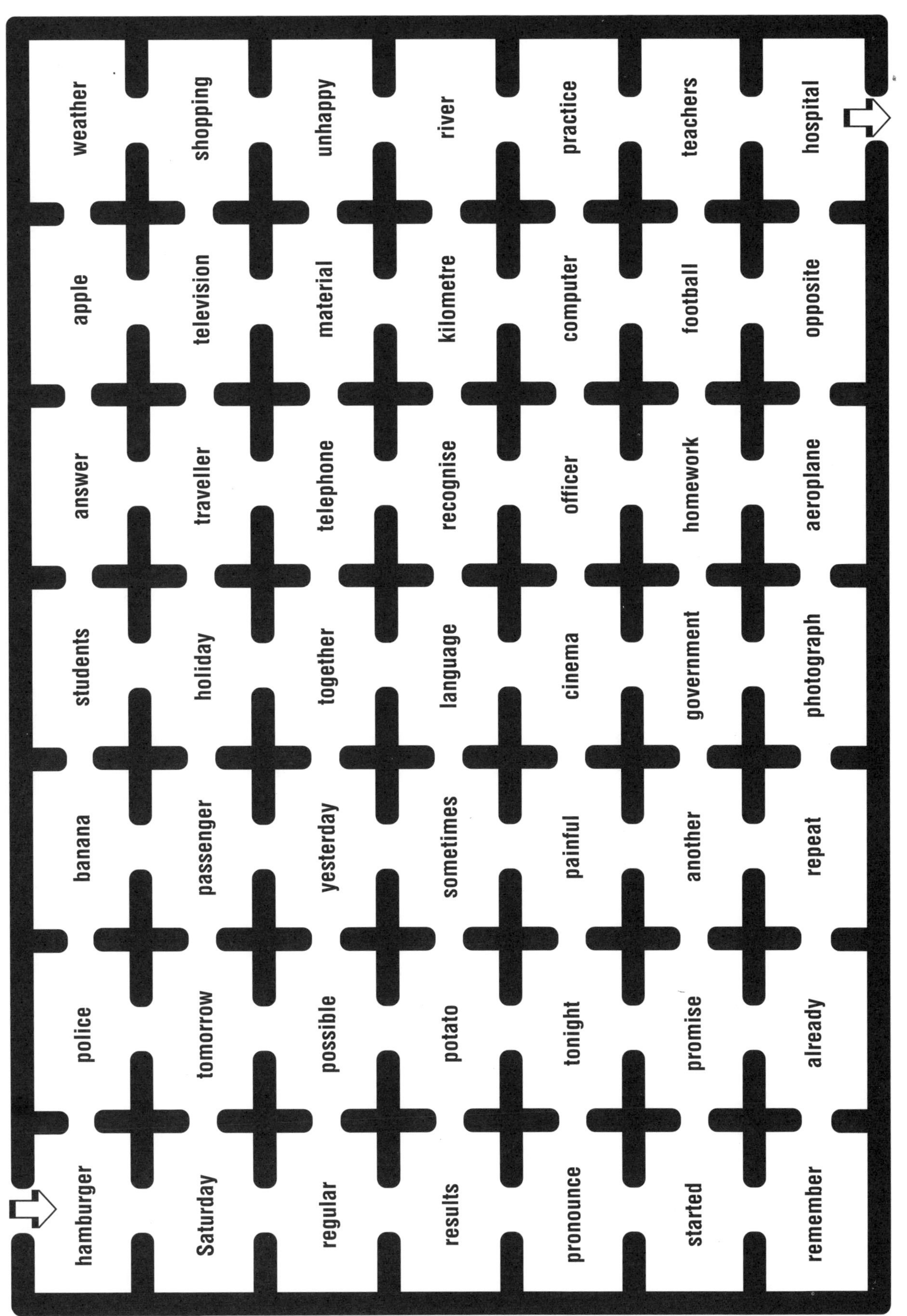

weather
shopping
unhappy
river
practice
teachers
hospital
apple
television
material
kilometre
computer
football
opposite
answer
traveller
telephone
recognise
officer
homework
aeroplane
students
holiday
together
language
cinema
government
photograph
banana
passenger
yesterday
sometimes
painful
another
repeat
police
tomorrow
possible
potato
tonight
promise
already
hamburger
Saturday
regular
results
pronounce
started
remember

Hidden names

B

Point: identifying the common sound in a group of words
Minimum level: intermediate
Game type: a look and find puzzle for students working individually (or in pairs)
Approximate time: 20 minutes

Preparation

Make a copy of the puzzle for each member of the class.

Presentation

1 Write the following words in a vertical column on the board and ask the class to identify what sound they all have in common:

eight rain face plate

2 Elicit that the sound in common is the vowel sound /eɪ/.

3 Try this exercise again with the following words:

races lose crazy rise

Elicit that the common sound here is the consonant /z/.

Conducting the game

1 Give each student a puzzle. (The game could also be played in pairs.) Explain that the names of the four members of the family in the pictures are hidden in the columns of words beside them.

2 To find the names, it is necessary to find the common sound that all the words in each column contain, then put these sounds together to make the name. If students are familiar with the phonetic script, it will be useful for noting down the common sound below each column. Otherwise, they will have to note it by underlining it in the words.

3 If necessary, work through the first name together as a class.

4 The game could be made easier by providing a 'menu' of possible names for the characters, such as:

Susan Michael Jenny Sarah Martin Charles Tony Jean Mark
Julian Sheila Sally David Matthew Shirley Joan Jane

Key

mother = Joan /dʒəʊn/

father = Charles /tʃɑːlz/

daughter = Sheila /ʃiːlə/

son = Matthew /mæθjuː/

Making your own versions

You can make other versions of this puzzle using other names, or in fact any words. Choose the name or word and note the sounds it contains. Find a group of four words that contain each sound (and no other) in common. Students in small groups could also make their own versions of the puzzle for their classmates to solve.

The names of the four people in this family are hidden in the words next to the pictures. Find the common sound in each list of words. Then join these sounds together to find the name.

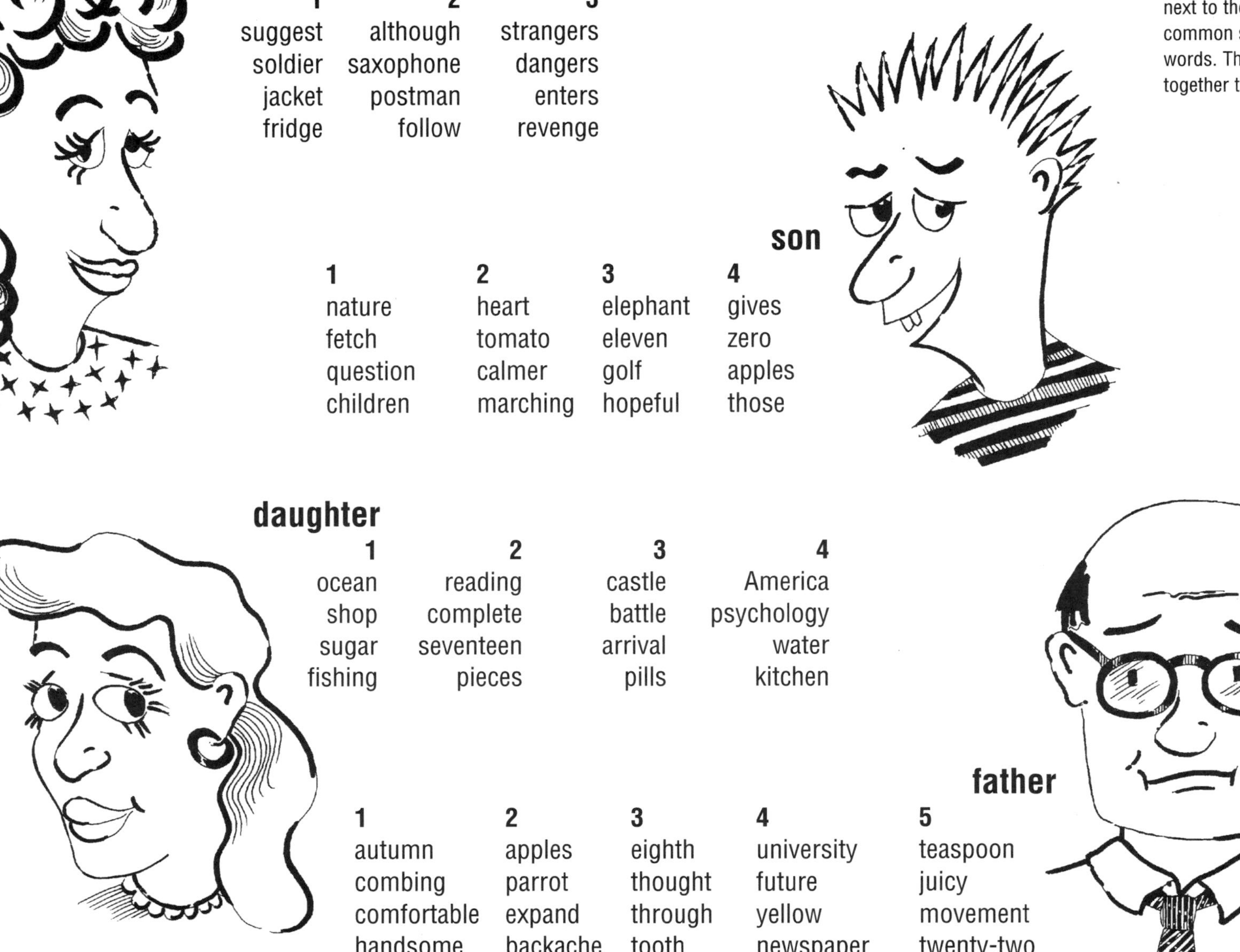

mother

1	2	3
suggest	although	strangers
soldier	saxophone	dangers
jacket	postman	enters
fridge	follow	revenge

son

1	2	3	4
nature	heart	elephant	gives
fetch	tomato	eleven	zero
question	calmer	golf	apples
children	marching	hopeful	those

daughter

1	2	3	4
ocean	reading	castle	America
shop	complete	battle	psychology
sugar	seventeen	arrival	water
fishing	pieces	pills	kitchen

father

1	2	3	4	5
autumn	apples	eighth	university	teaspoon
combing	parrot	thought	future	juicy
comfortable	expand	through	yellow	movement
handsome	backache	tooth	newspaper	twenty-two

Pronunciation journey

B

Point: minimal pairs
Minimum level: elementary
Game type: a listen and respond game for the whole class
Approximate time: 15 minutes

Preparation

Make a copy of the map for each member of the class. Then choose some pairs of words from your course. The word pairs should differ in only one sound. Here are some examples:

men/man place/plays taught/thought ship/sheep

There are several published books giving lists of these minimal pairs. For this game, you need four pairs of words.

Presentation

1 Write the word pairs in two vertical columns on the board. Label the lists *left* and *right*.

left	**right**
men	man
place	plays
taught	thought
ship	sheep

2 Read out words from the board in random order and ask students to say which list they are from.

Conducting the game

1 Give each student a map. Point out that at each of the numbered junctions, there is a choice of turning left or right.

2 Explain that you will read four words from the board, one word for each junction. For each word, students must turn left or right according to whether the word is from the left or the right hand list on the board. When you have said the four words, students should then arrive at one of the destinations along the top of the map. For example:

men - place - thought - ship → Singapore

3 Go over the route together to check the correct route.

4 Repeat the activity several times using the same four pairs of words or using other minimal pairs.

5 Students can play the game in pairs or small groups. They take turns to read out words and trace the route on the map.

Pronunciation journey B2

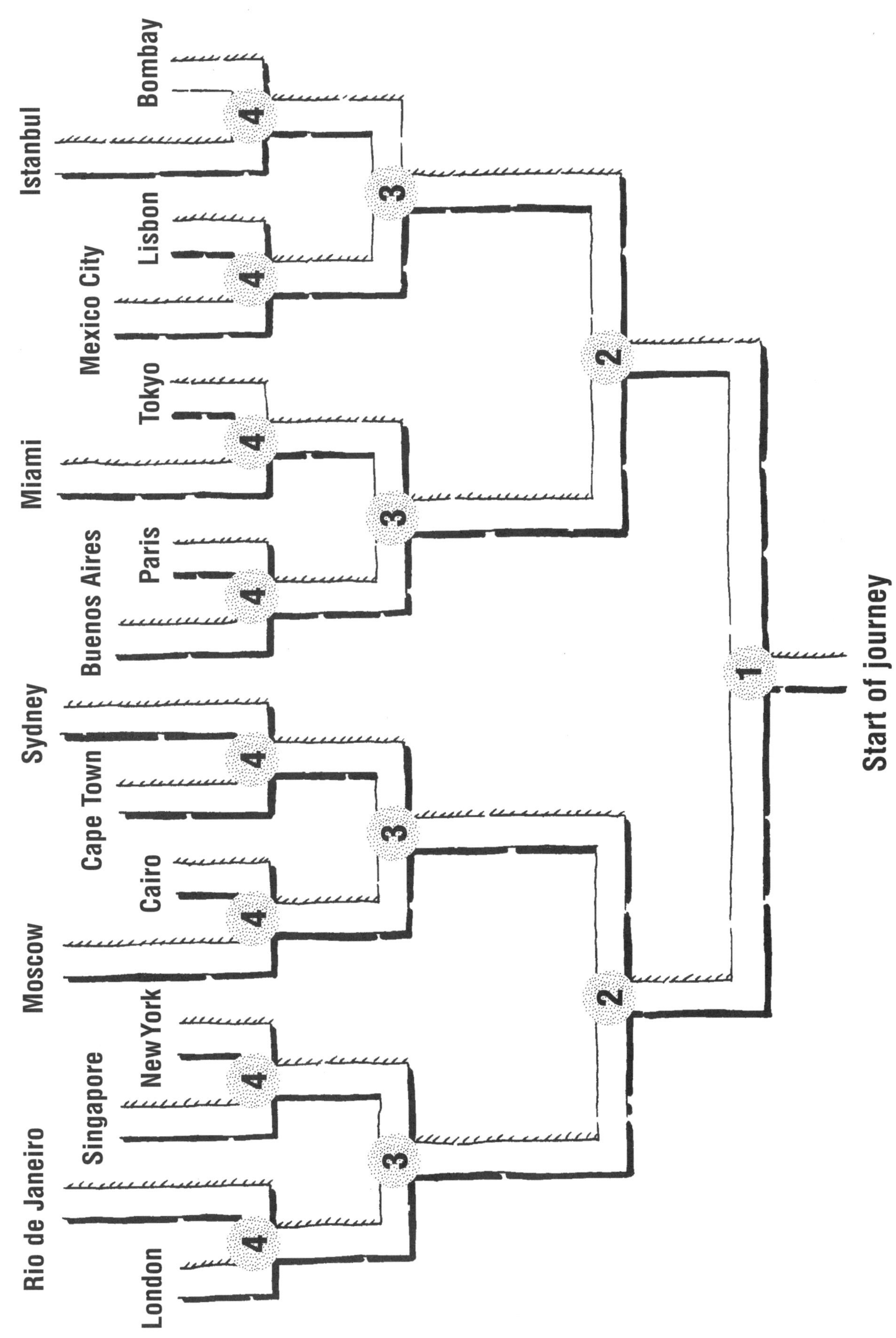

Four-sided dominoes

B

Point: matching vowel sounds
Minimum level: pre-intermediate
Game type: a matching card game for three players
Approximate time: 30 minutes

Rules

1 Play this game in pairs or groups of three. Make one player responsible for keeping the score. Deal the same number of cards to each player. If you are playing in a group of three, place one card in the middle as a starter and put the other card to one side.

2 Take turns to place cards on the table and build a track. You must place one of your cards so that it touches one of the sides of the last card that was placed on the table. The words in the sides that are next to each other must contain the same vowel sound.

3 After each turn, the scorekeeper writes the score. You score: *1* point for placing a card correctly, *1* point for saying which vowel sound is the same in the words that are touching, *0* points for placing a card incorrectly. You must then take your card back and miss a turn.

4 A player who is unable to place a card when it is his or her turn, misses that turn.

5 When one player has placed all his or her cards, the scorekeeper adds up everyone's total score; the player with most points is the winner.

Preparation

Copy and cut out a set of cards for each group of three students in the class.

Presentation

1 Write the following words on the board as examples of words containing the eight vowel sounds in this game:

1 sing /ɪ/ **2** men /e/ **3** rice /aɪ/ **4** sun /ʌ/ **5** rain /eɪ/ **6** eat /iː/ **7** go /əʊ/ **8** had /æ/

2 Ask students to suggest other one-syllable words that contain the eight vowel sounds.

Conducting the game

1 Divide the class into groups of three and give each group a pack of cards. (The game could also be played in pairs.)

2 Explain and/or give out the rules.

3 During the game, move around the class helping students to resolve any disputes. Check that the words are correctly matched on the cards. Alternatively, give a copy of the key to each group so that they can check for themselves, or ask students to check the words in the dictionary.

Follow-up

A possible follow-up would be for each group to choose one of the eight vowel sounds and note down all the ways it can be spelt in the words on the cards. If you have distributed the key, a glance at this will make it plain that there are a range of possible spellings for each sound.

Key

1 /ɪ/ big, build, film, give, his, live, sing, sit, this, with

2 /e/ bed, bread, dead, head, leg, pet, said, ten, then, went

3 /aɪ/ cry, five, like, light, nice, side, time, tried, white, write

4 /ʌ/ blood, but, come, cup, cut, fun, some, son, won, young

5 /eɪ/ day, eight, gave, great, late, made, name, pain, they, wake

6 /iː/ be, beach, key, leave, sea, see, ski, these, tree, week

7 /əʊ/ both, know, no, old, phone, road, show, smoke, so, toe

8 /æ/ bad, can, cat, catch, fat, hand, have, man, match, sad

Rules

1 Play this game in pairs or groups of three. Make one player responsible for keeping the score. Deal the same number of cards to each player. If you are playing in a group of three, place one card in the middle as a starter and put the other card to one side.

2 Take turns to place cards on the table and build a track. You must place one of your cards so that it touches one of the sides of the last card that was placed on the table. The words in the sides that are next to each other must contain the same vowel sound.

3 After each turn, the scorekeeper writes the score. You score:
1 point for placing a card correctly,
1 point for saying which vowel sound is the same in the words that are touching,
0 points for placing a card incorrectly. You must then take your card back and miss a turn.

4 A player who is unable to place a card when it is his or her turn, misses that turn.

5 When one player has placed all his or her cards, the scorekeeper adds up everyone's total score; the player with most points is the winner.

Card	Top	Left	Right	Bottom
1	bread	this	ski	have
2	give	build	late	see
3	sit	toe	match	live
4	bed	went	fat	phone
5	sing	cut	road	fun
6	pet	great	both	head
7	side	hand	white	dead
8	smoke	five	cry	made
9	won	be	tree	film
10	then	some	but	man
11	name	like	gave	cat
12	son	sad	day	time
13	beach	wake	eight	big
14	bad	week	pain	said
15	these	nice	leave	so
16	light	cup	know	no
17	his	come	show	sea
18	old	they	can	ten
19	key	catch	young	write
20	with	leg	tried	blood

Sound pictures

B

Point: awareness of sounds
Minimum level: pre-intermediate
Game type: a find-the-difference puzzle for students working in pairs
Approximate time: 15 minutes

Preparation

Copy a picture pair for each pair of students in your class. You may also want to make a copy on an OHP transparency or a large piece of paper.

Conducting the game

1 Divide the class into pairs. Give one member of each pair picture a and give the other member picture b. Ask students to describe the pictures carefully to each other and find the differences between them. (They should not look at each other's pictures.) Alternatively, give out picture a first, collect it in and then give out picture b. In this case, students should identify the differences from memory.
2 Divide the board into two columns, one for each of the two sounds in the picture pair. At the top of each column write the phonetic symbol for the sound and/or an example of a word containing the sound. Ask members of the class to call out the differences they have discovered. For each difference, there should be one key word that contains one of the two sounds. Repeat this word and ask students to say which of the columns it should go in.
3 Finally, allow students to look at the pictures again and ask them to find any other examples of words with one of the two sounds in them.

Key

The key sounds for each pair of pictures are given along with the words that students will need to use when identifying the differences between the pictures.
(The words in brackets refer to items in both pictures.)

Pair 1	/eɪ/	ace, label, radio, railway, suitcase, table, train, weight (cake, ice skates, plate, rain, tape)
	/aɪ/	kite, light, mice, pipe, type-writer, wine (bike, ice skates, night, sign, sky)
Pair 2	/əʊ/	banjo, bowl, comb, hole, loaf, rope, saxophone, sofa, telephone, toast, toaster
	/uː/	boots, newspaper, moon, soup, spoon (flute, fruit, glue, roof, ruler)
Pair 3	/ɒ/	clock, dog, golf clubs, lock, salt, sausages, socks, swan, washing machine, yacht (bomb, bottle, box, orange, teapot)
	/ʌ/	cup, duck, gloves, golf clubs, gun, monkey, mug, skull (dove, drum, jug, sun)
Pair 4	/iː/	fields, meat, sheep, teapot, teeth, trees (beach, feet, knee, sea)
	/ɪ/	chin, cigarette, finger, fish, guitar, lips, picture, pig, violin, window (drink, hill, river)
Pair 5	/dʒ/	bridge, giraffe, jacket, jet, jug, message, orange (cage, fridge)
	/tʃ/	chair, cheese, chicken, church, matches, picture, vulture (chocolate)

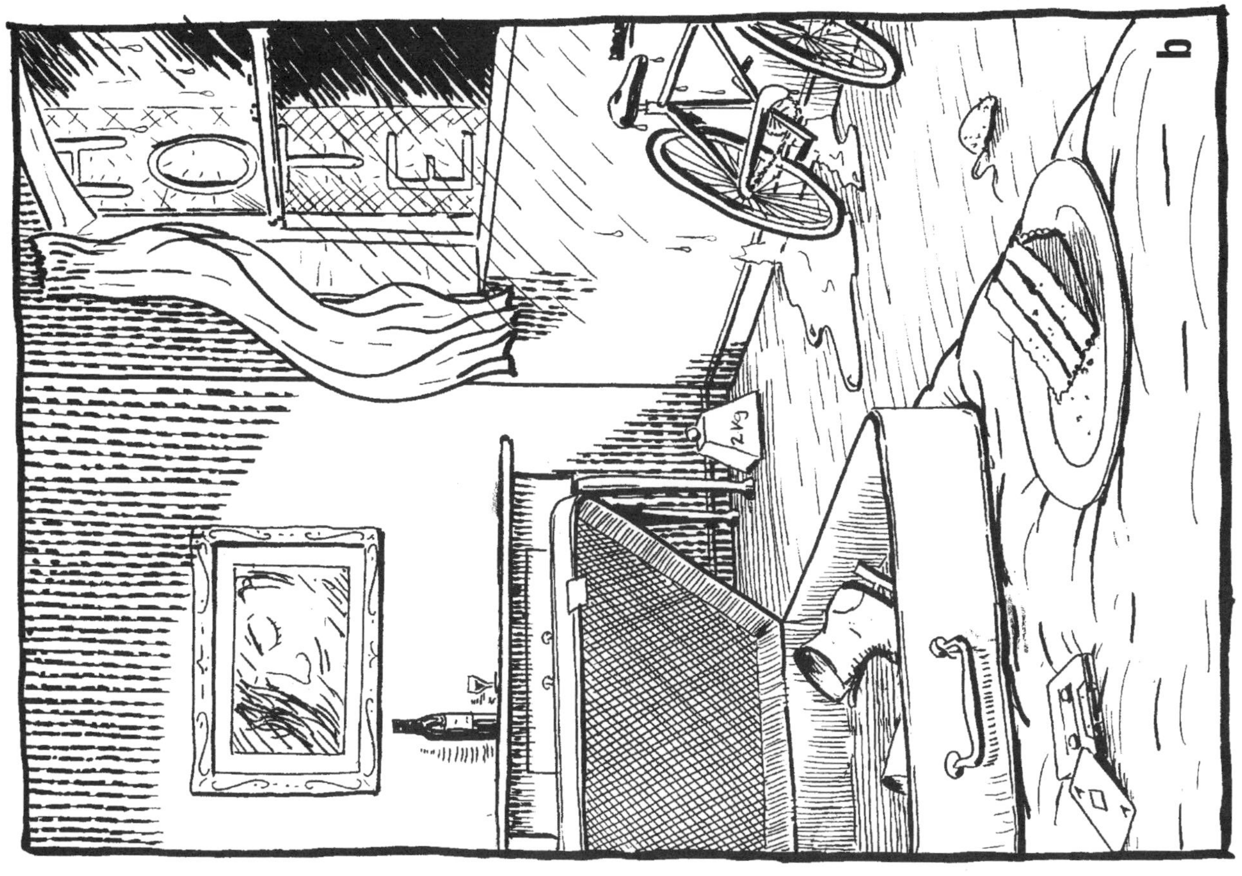
b
2kg

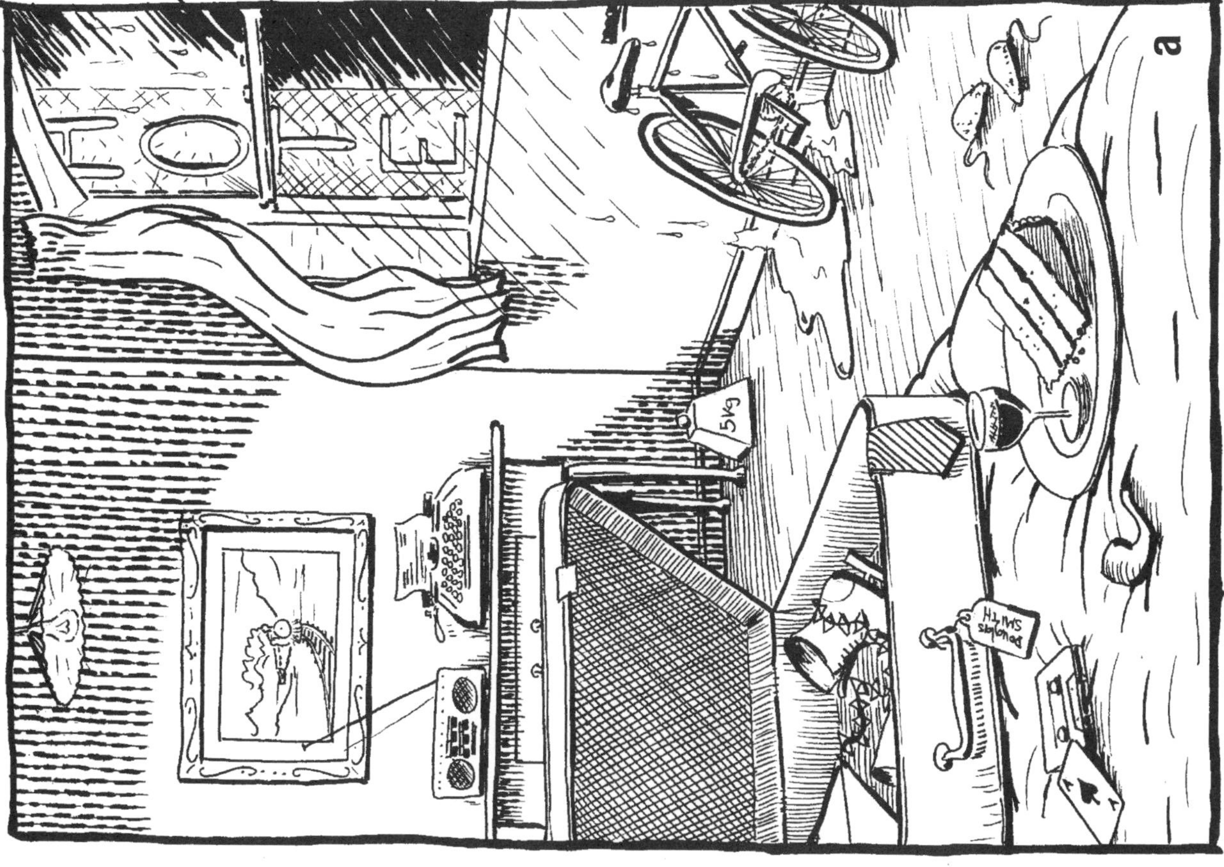
a
5kg

B4 Sound pictures Pair 2

b

a

B4 Sound pictures Pair 4

SUPER FREEZE
b

SUPER FREEZE
a

Win a word

B

Point: vowel sounds in words spelt with a final *e*
Minimum level: intermediate
Game type: a matching card game for three players
Approximate time: 20 minutes

Rules

1 Divide the cards equally among the players. The aim of the game is to win as many of the cards as possible.

2 Players take turns to place cards on the table.

3 There should be two piles, one for word beginnings and one for word endings. All the word endings end with an *e* and are in a shape pointing to the right. Word beginnings are in a shape pointing left. For example:

word beginning   word ending

ma   **de**

4 Players continue placing cards on the two piles. If, at any point, the beginning and the ending form a word, the first player to notice this must put a hand over the cards and say the word.

5 All the players must decide together if this word exists; if they are not sure, they may ask the player who said the word to say what it means and then check it in a dictionary. If the word exists, this player then wins all the cards in the piles. Players should make a note of all the words that come up during the game.

6 The game continues until all the cards that were dealt out at the beginning have been played. The player with most cards at this point is the winner.

Preparation

Copy and cut out a set of cards for each group of three students in your class.

Presentation

1 The vowel in one-syllable words with a final silent *e* tends to be pronounced as it is in the alphabet. So, for example, the *a* in *rate* is pronounced like the letter *A* when reciting the alphabet, that is, /eɪ/. To illustrate this point, write the following words on the board:

rat pet sit not cut

Demonstrate how the pronunciation of these words changes with the addition of a final *e* to:

rate /reɪt/ Pete /piːt/ site /saɪt/ note /nəʊt/ cute /kjuːt/

Show that the written vowel in the middle of these words is pronounced as the letter in the alphabet:

a = /eɪ/ e = /iː/ i = /aɪ/ o = /əʊ/ u = /juː/

2 Ask students to predict how the following words might be pronounced:

kale mace swede cline splice lode rote mule

(Note that *u* may also be pronounced /uː/ as in *flute*.)

Conducting the game

1 Divide the class into groups of three and give each group a pack of cards. (The game could also be played in pairs.)

2 Explain and/or give out the rules.

3 During the game, move around the class helping students to resolve any disputes. Ask players to pronounce the words that they have written down.

Key

fa - face fade fake fame fate

ho - hole home hope hose

la - lace lake lame lane late

li - lice like lime line

ma - mace made make male mate

ro - robe rode role Rome rope rose

ru - rude rule

the - theme these

ti - tide tile time

wi - wide wine wipe wise

Win a word B5

Rules

1 Divide the cards equally among the players. The aim of the game is to win as many of the cards as possible.

2 Players take turns to place cards on the table.

3 There should be two piles, one for word beginnings and one for word endings. All the word endings end with an *e* and are in a shape pointing to the right. Word beginnings are in a shape pointing left. For example:

word beginning	word ending
ma	de

4 Players continue placing cards on the two piles. If, at any point, the beginning and the ending form a word, the first player to notice this must put a hand over the cards and say the word.

5 All the players must decide together if this word exists; if they are not sure, they may ask the player who said the word to say what it means and then check it in a dictionary. If the word exists, this player then wins all the cards in the piles. Players should make a note of all the words that come up during the game.

6 The game continues until all the cards that were dealt out at the beginning have been played. The player with most cards at this point is the winner.

fa	la	me	se
ma	the	de	ce
wi	ti	ke	le
li	ro	ne	be
ho	ru	te	pe

Ludo

B

Point: vowels followed by a written *r* (game 1); consonant sounds (game 2)
Minimum level: intermediate
Game type: a racing game with dice and board for three or four players
Approximate time: 45 minutes

Rules

1 Place your counters on the starting position (the outer triangles marked A, B, C and D). The object of the game is to go around the board to the finishing position (the inner triangles marked A, B, C and D). The first player to do this is the winner.

2 Go around the board in the direction shown by the arrow in your starting triangle and do not cross any thick lines.

3 Take turns to throw the dice and move. To move, check the dice next to the board to find out which sound is indicated by the number on the dice:

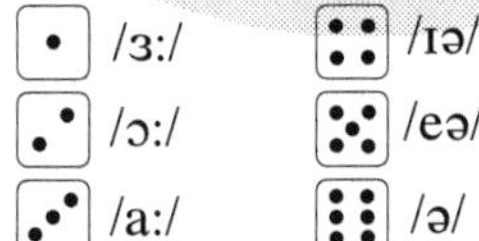

Then move around the board to the first word containing that sound. If the other players agree that you have moved your counter to a word which does not contain the sound that you are looking for, put your counter back where it was and miss a turn.

4 When there are no more words on the board which contain the sound that you are looking for, move directly to the finishing position.

5 If another player lands on the square where your counter is, miss a turn.

Preparation

Make a copy of the board and provide a dice for each group of three or four students in the class. Provide a counter for each student.

Presentation

1 Write the following words on the board:

head spot had bee pea late

Ask students to add the letter *r* after a vowel in each of these words to make another word. Write the words on the board:

heard sport hard beer pear later

These words illustrate the six vowel sounds which tend to result when a vowel is followed by the letter *r*, ie:

heard	sport	hard	beer	pear	later
/hɜ:d/	/spɔ:t/	/ha:d/	/bɪə/	/peə/	/leɪtə/
/ɜ:/	/ɔ:/	/a:/	/ɪə/	/eə/	/ə/

As the above transcriptions make clear, the *r* itself may be completely silent.

2 Write the following table on the board to illustrate the six vowel sounds that result when the letter *r* follows a vowel. (Include the bracketed words in the table only with more advanced classes.)

1 /ɜ:/	**2** /ɔ:/	**3** /a:/	**4** /ɪə/	**5** /eə/	**6** /ə/
bird	bored	(barred)	beard	(bared)	border
(burr)	bore	bar	beer	bear	(bearer)
er...	or	are	ear	air	error
fur	four	far	fear	fair	fairer
were	war		we're	wear	wearer

(Note that the words in each row differ only in the vowel sound in columns 1-5; these words are minimal pairs.) Column 6 is included to show the sound /ə/ in the second syllable.

3 Model the pronunciation of the words in the table, then read words from it at random and ask the class to say which column the word comes from. Then ask students to read out words for their classmates to identify the column.

Conducting the game

1 Divide the class into groups of three or four and give each group a board, a dice and counters.
2 Explain that the numbers on the dice correspond to the six sounds along the top of the table on the board.
3 Explain the rules and/or give out the rules sheets. You could advise the players to consult dictionaries in case of doubts.

Ludo

B

Key Game 1

1/ɜː/	**2**/ɔː/	**3**/aː/	**4**/ɪə/	**5**/eə/	**6**/ə/
bird	bored	are	beard	air	colour
earth	door	arm	beer	bear	doctor
first	four	art	cheer	care	figure
girl	more	car	dear	chair	later
her	pour	dark	hear	there	mother
turn	sport	hard	here	wear	picture
were	war	heart	near	where	sugar
word					
work					

Follow-up

A second version of the game which concentrates on six consonant sounds is also included. The numbers on the dice in this game correspond to the sounds as follows;

1 /t/ (teach) **2** /tʃ/ (cheap) **3** /dʒ/ (age) **4** /s/ (see) **5** /z/ (zoo) **6** /ʃ/ (shoe)

Key Game 2

1 /t/	**2** /tʃ/	**3** /dʒ/	**4** /s/	**5** /z/	**6** /ʃ/
acting	catch	bridge	aches	easy	action
hoped	chair	cage	grocer	exam	luxury
liked	chip	joke	loose	lose	nation
native	lecture	June	mix	news	ocean
pattern	peach	orange	passing	pays	passion
turn	picture	page	place	plays	patient
what	watch		rice	rise	shop
	which		sore		sure

B6 Ludo Game 1

Rules

1 Place your counters on the starting position (the outer triangles marked A, B, C and D). The object of the game is to go around the board to the finishing position (the inner triangles marked A, B, C and D). The first player to do this is the winner.

2 Go around the board in the direction shown by the arrow in your starting triangle and do not cross any thick lines.

3 Take turns to throw the dice and move. To move, check the dice next to the board to find out which sound is indicated by the number on the dice:

Dice	Sound	Dice	Sound
⚀	/ɜː/	⚃	/ɪə/
⚁	/ɔː/	⚄	/eə/
⚂	/ɑː/	⚅	/ə/

Then move around the board to the first word containing that sound. If the other players agree that you have moved your counter to a word which does not contain the sound that you are looking for, put your counter back where it was and miss a turn.

4 When there are no more words on the board which contain the sound that you are looking for, move directly to the finishing position.

5 If another player lands on the square where your counter is, miss a turn.

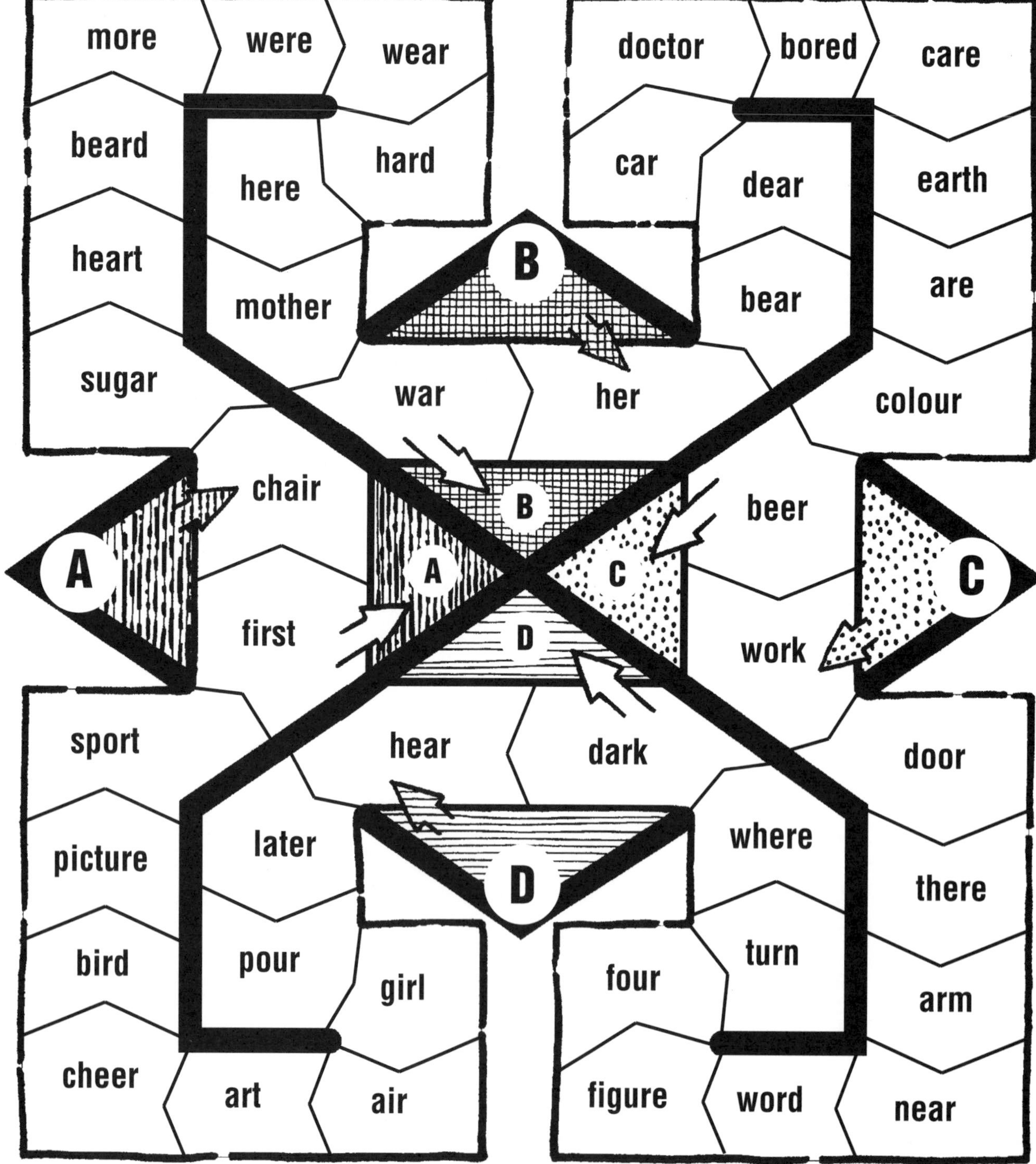

Rules

1 Place your counters on the starting position (the outer triangles marked A, B, C and D). The object of the game is to go around the board to the finishing position (the inner triangles marked A, B, C and D). The first player to do this is the winner.

2 Go around the board in the direction shown by the arrow in your starting triangle and do not cross any thick lines.

3 Take turns to throw the dice and move. To move, check the dice next to the board to find out which sound is indicated by the number on the dice:

- ⚀ /t/
- ⚁ /tʃ/
- ⚂ /dʒ/
- ⚃ /s/
- ⚄ /z/
- ⚅ /ʃ/

Then move around the board to the first word containing that sound. If the other players agree that you have moved your counter to a word which does not contain the sound that you are looking for, put your counter back where it was and miss a turn.

4 When there are no more words on the board which contain the sound that you are looking for, move directly to the finishing position.

5 If another player lands on the square where your counter is, miss a turn.

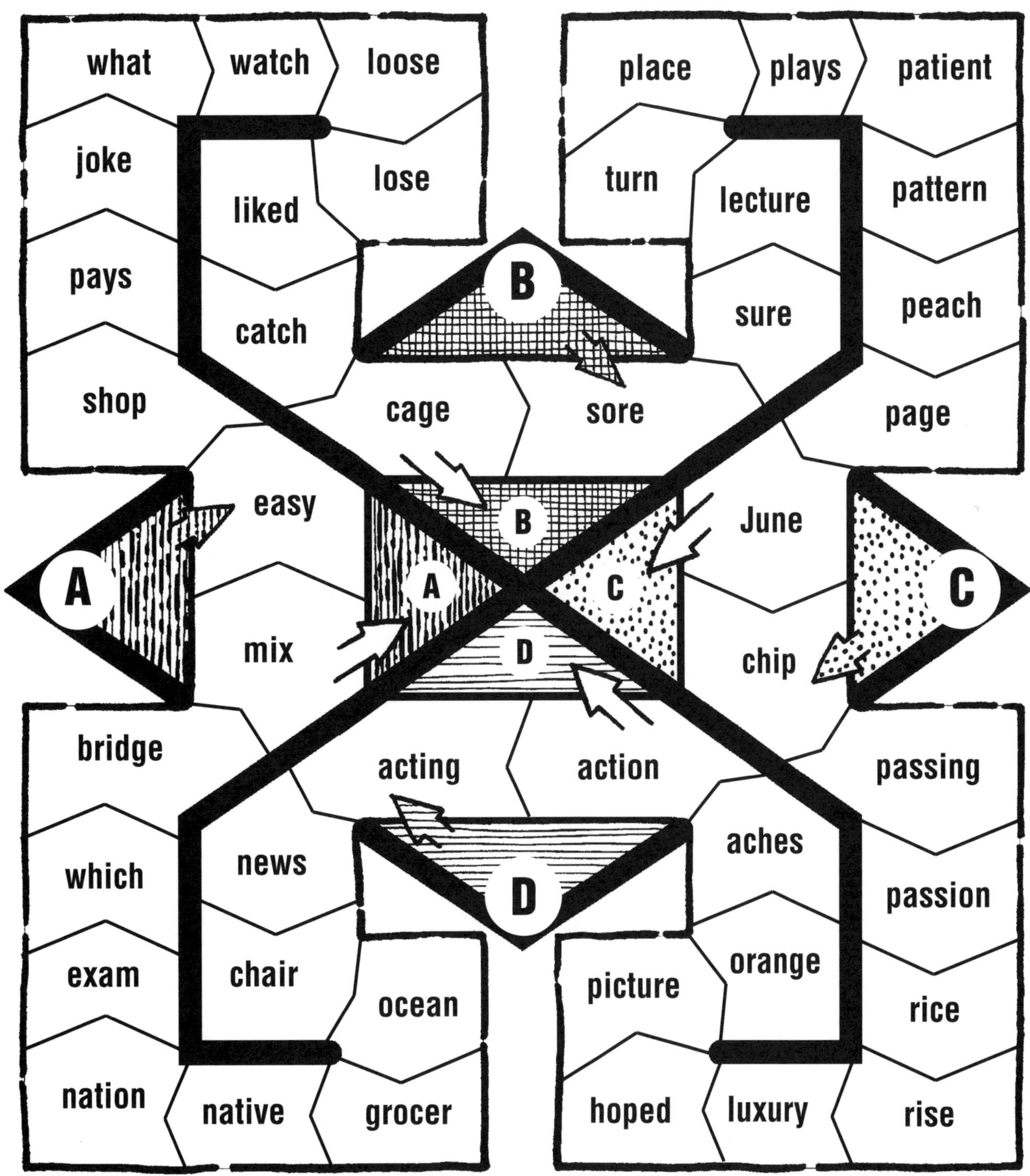

B Two-vowel jigsaw

Point: pairs of written vowels
Minimum level: elementary
Game type: a matching puzzle for students working individually (or in pairs)
Approximate time: 20 minutes

Preparation

Copy and cut out a set of cards for each pair of students in the class. Cut across the thick line and along the dotted lines only. It is easiest to begin by cutting the vertical lines, and cut the horizontal lines afterwards. There are two different puzzles, one with words containing the letters *ea* and another with words containing the letters *oo* and *ou*.

Conducting the game

1 Divide the class into pairs and give each pair a pack of cards. Explain that the idea of the game is for students to put the pieces of the puzzle together so that words are formed within the rectangle.
2 Explain that the double line is the outside edge of the puzzle.
3 While students are working on the puzzle, write on the board the phonetic symbol and an example word for each of the vowel sounds in the puzzle. (See key.) Draw a column beneath each symbol.
4 As students finish the puzzle, ask them to copy what you have written on the board and write the words from the game in the appropriate column according to the pronunciation of the vowel in the word. If they are unsure, advise them to consult a dictionary. You might like to point out that three of the words in the first puzzle (*lead, read, tear*) can be pronounced in two different ways and therefore belong in two different lists on the board.
5 Finally, check answers with the class and drill the pronunciation.

Key

Puzzle 1 (words with *ea*)

/iː/	/e/	/eə/	/ɪə/	/eɪ/
beat	bread	bear	dear	break
cheat	dead	tear	hear	steak
heat	head	wear	near	
lead	lead		tear	
mean	read			
meat				
peace				
please				
read				

(Note that *lead, read* and *tear* can be pronounced in two different ways.)

Puzzle 2 (words with *oo* and *ou*)

/aʊ/	/ʊ/	/uː/	/ɔː/	/ʌ/
found	could	boot	bought	country
house	foot	food	door	touch
mouth	good	group	four	
sound	look	moon		
	wood	school		
	would			

steak	read	dear	mean	heat
dead	please	break	peace	cheat
hear	bread	bear	lead	near
beat	head	wear	meat	tear

B7 Two-vowel jigsaw Puzzle 2

bought food door moon look

group foot boot would school

good sound wood found could

house touch mouth country four

Simple sound maze

8B

Point: individual sound /iː/ (puzzle 1); individual sound /jː/ (puzzle 2)
Minimum level: elementary
Game type: a path-finding puzzle for students working individually (or in pairs)
Approximate time: 15 minutes

Preparation

Make a copy of the maze for each member of the class.

Conducting the game

1 Give each student a maze. (The game could also be played in pairs.)
2 Explain that the object of the game is to find a path from the entrance in the top left side of the maze to the exit in the bottom right.
3 Point out the phonetic symbol and example word above the maze and explain that in the game, you can only cross a square if it contains a word with that sound.
4 You can move from one square to the next horizontally or vertically, but not diagonally.
5 When students have finished, check the route together.
6 If your students are familiar with phonetic script, ask them to transcribe the words in the correct path, perhaps for homework.

Key **Puzzle 1**

The correct path is:

tea - these - meat - meet - complete - need - eat - sheep - scene - TV - feel - seat - read - please - street - me - sea - cheap - feet - bean - teach - tree - east - meal

Making your own versions

You can make other versions of the maze, concentrating on other sounds or on vocabulary from your course. Make a list of about 25 words with one particular sound and write them in the grid so that they form a continuous path from entry to exit. Then make another list of words that do not contain the sound but look as if they could. Write these in the remaining squares.

Follow-up

A grid of hexagons could equally well be used and an example is included here which concentrates on the sound /j/. This maze is suitable for advanced learners. (Note that this maze will not work for American English.)

Key **Puzzle 2**

The correct path is:

young - uniform - new - argue - union - unit - futile - view - use - confuse - duty - usual - year - future - utopia - tutor - revenue - universe - youth

The following words also contain the sound /j/:

you - yet - few - yes - tune

B8 Simple sound maze **Puzzle 1** /i:/ (see)

tea	these	meat	meet	main
like	this	friend	complete	hear
scene	sheep	eat	need	fit
TV	ship	it	year	pain
feel	fill	night	head	fly
seat	read	please	right	fine
sit	dead	street	break	smile
cheap	sea	me	fight	sin
feet	bear	beer	nine	sign
bean	teach	tree	east	meal

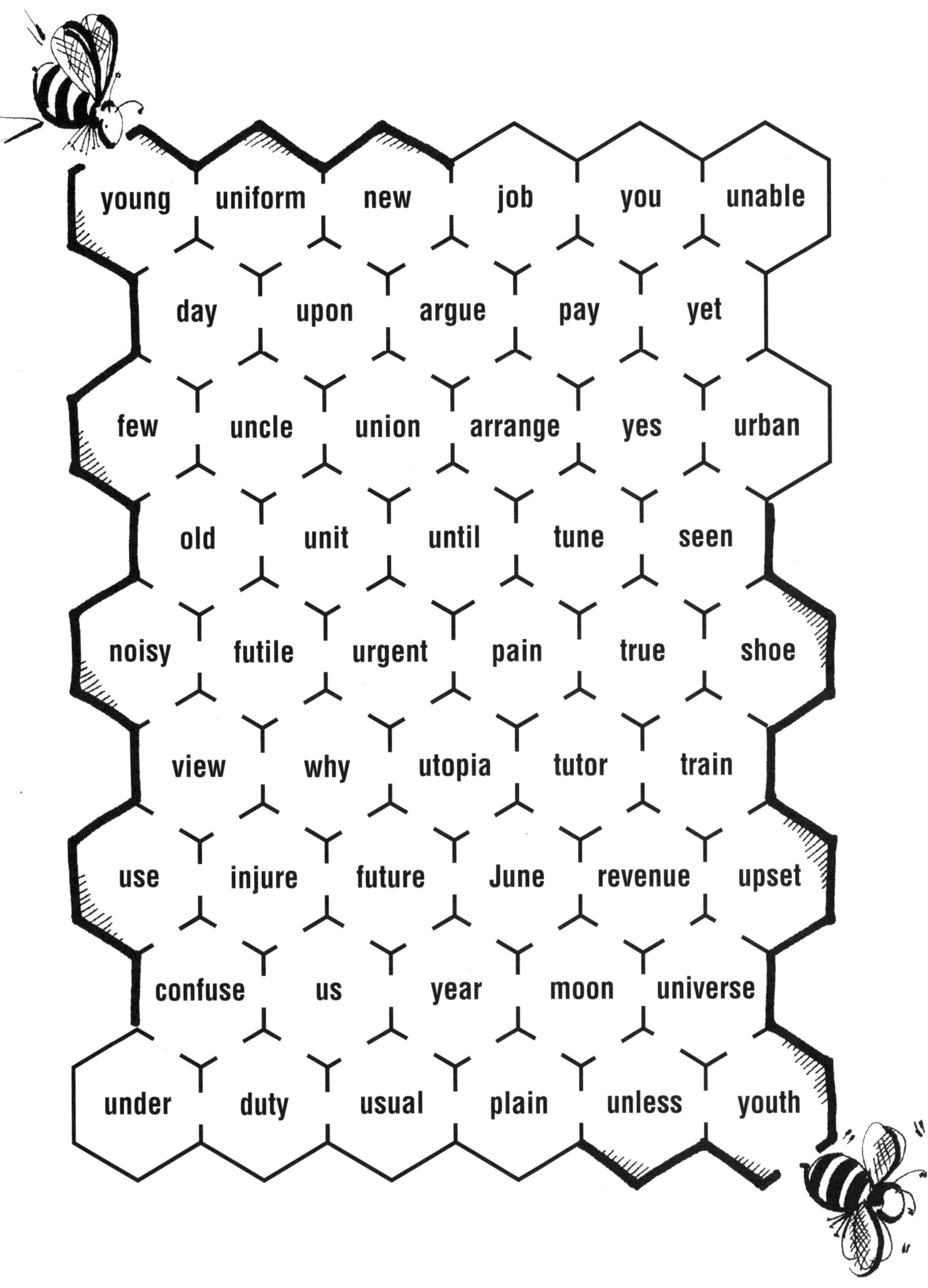
young
uniform
new
job
you
unable
day
upon
argue
pay
yet
few
uncle
union
arrange
yes
urban
old
unit
until
tune
seen
noisy
futile
urgent
pain
true
shoe
view
why
utopia
tutor
train
use
injure
future
June
revenue
upset
confuse
us
year
moon
universe
under
duty
usual
plain
unless
youth

Complex sound maze

B 9

Point: individual sounds *a, e, i, o, u* as pronounced in the alphabet (puzzle 1); rhyming words (puzzle 2)
Minimum level: intermediate
Game type: a path-finding puzzle for students working individually (or in pairs)
Approximate time: 20 minutes

Preparation

Make a copy of the maze for each member of the class.

Conducting the game

1 Give each student a maze. (The game could also be played in pairs.)
2 Explain that the object of the game is to find a path from the entrance in the top left side of the grid to the exit in the bottom right.
3 Write on the board the letters *a, e, i, o* and *u* and elicit how they are pronounced in reciting the alphabet, ie /eɪ/, /iː/, /aɪ/, /əʊ/, /juː/. Ask students to find an example of a word containing each of the sounds.
4 You can only move from one box to another if one of the two words in each box shares the same vowel sound. It does not matter if you use the upper or the lower word in the box.
5 You can move from one square to the next horizontally or vertically, but not diagonally.
6 When students have finished, check the route together.
7 If your students are familiar with phonetic script, ask them to transcribe the words in the correct path, perhaps for homework.

Key **Puzzle 1**

The correct path is:

same - main - gave/need - cheap - see/light - side - white - sky - like/home - boat - coach - no/use - view - few/teach - green - scene/wife - try - time - right - high/page - wait - cake - rain/road - woke - toast - smoke/please - meet

Follow-up

Ask students to identify any spelling patterns in the words in the maze. They might identify for each sound a spelling consisting of two written vowels and another with a final silent *e* as in the following examples:

/eɪ/ - paid, same /iː/ - need, scene /aɪ/ - tie, five /əʊ/ - boat, woke /juː/ - view, use

Making your own versions

You may want to make your own versions of the maze with vocabulary from your course. To do this, construct a path of words that have sounds in common in adjacent squares from entry to exit. Then fill in the remaining squares with other words. Make sure that these distractors do not contain sounds which can be found in squares adjacent to the path.

A grid of hexagons could equally well be used and an example is included here which concentrates on rhyming words, eg *feet, heat, meet, neat, seat.* This maze is suitable for pre-intermediate students.

Key **Puzzle 2**

The correct path is:

meet - eat/do - new - you - two/socks - box/no - toe - know/what - got/come - mum/see - me/wait - late - eight/ear - hear/bring - sing/put - foot/good - wood/pen - men/pretty - city/hair - there/eye - my/your - four/right - kite/car - are/fine - nine

Puzzle 1 (a, e, i, o, u) Complex sound maze

B9

same	main	need	June	see	youth	day
why	tube	gave	cheap	light	tune	save
queen	home	sky	white	knew	rain	tie
bean	like	news	road	side	road	woke
plane	boat	pain	peace	wait	cake	you
five	mean	coach	these	know	nice	toast
teach	view	use	wrote	high	need	smoke
few	wake	no	right	page	leave	please
green	wife	try	eat	hope	coat	line
paid	scene	sale	time	show	please	meet

B9 Complex sound maze **Puzzle 2** (rhyming words)

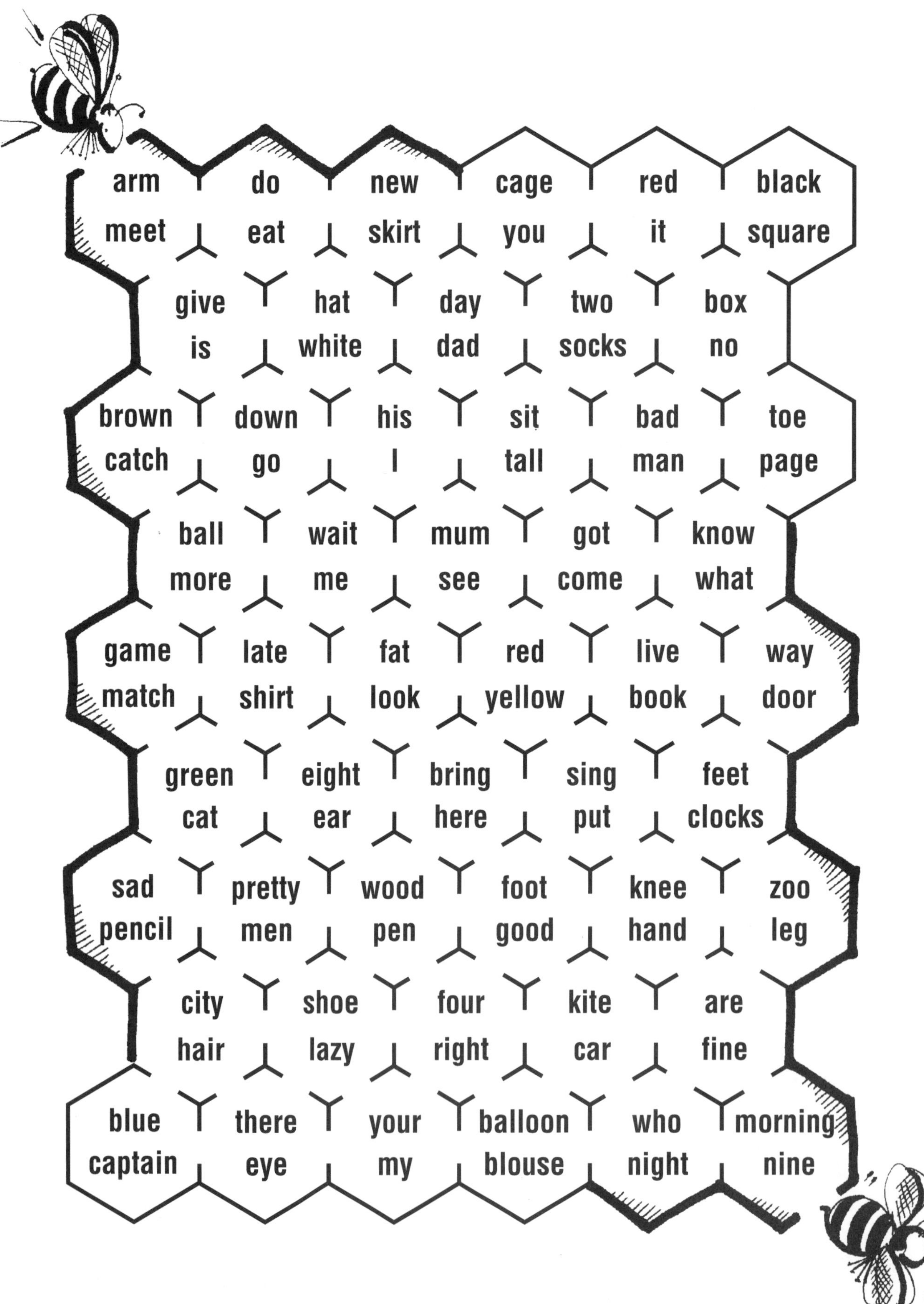

10 Battleships

Point: sounds and phonetic symbols
Minimum level: pre-intermediate
Game type: a guessing game for two players
Approximate time: 20 minutes

Rules

1 Draw two ships on your map making sure that nobody sees where you have put your ships. You may put your ships inside any square where there is sea (white on the map). Your ships must not cross a line into another square.

2 Work in pairs. The object of the game is to guess where the other player has put the ships and bomb them.

3 To do this, decide which square to bomb and make a word out of the sounds at the side of the map. In game 1, for example, if the square you want to bomb is in the column with the sound /t/ and the row /iː/, say *tea*. In game 2, for example, if the square you want to bomb is in the row with the sound /k/ and the column with the sound /iːz/, say *keys*.

4 If the square that you bomb contains a ship, the other player must say *hit*. If the square that you bomb is next to a square with a ship in it (including diagonally), the other player must say *near*.

5 Players take turns to bomb each other's ships and the first person to hit both of the other player's ships is the winner.

6 A player whose ship is being bombed may challenge the other player to spell the word that he or she is saying; if the other player is unable to spell the word, he or she misses a turn.

Preparation

Make a copy of the map for each member of the class. Note that two different maps for two different games are included.

Conducting the game

1 Give each student a map. Model the pronunciation of the words around the side of the map.
2 Divide the class into pairs.
3 Explain and/or give out the rules.
4 Players who finish quickly can be asked to try and write the words in each of the sea squares on the map.

Key

Map 1

ʃ	h	b	t	p	d	f	w	
-	-	boy	toy	-	-	-	-	ɔɪ
-	-	bore	tore	pour	door	for/ four	war/ wore	ɔː
-	here/ hear	beer	tear/ tier	pier	dear/ deer	fear	-	ɪə
share	hair	bare/ bear	tear	pear/ pair	dare	fair/ fare	wear/ where	eə
shy	high	buy/by	tie	pie	die	-	why	aɪ
she	he	be/bee	tea	pea	-	-	we	iː

Map 2

	ɪn	ɪŋ	ɪk	ɔːt	iːz	eəz	əʊz	æt
s	sin	sing	sick	sort	seas/ sees/ seize	-	sews	sat
k	kin	king	kick	caught/ court	keys	cares	-	cat
tʃ	chin	-	chick	-	cheese	chairs	chose	chat
ð	-	-	-	-	these	theirs/ there's	those	that
ʃ	-	-	-	short	she's	shares	shows	-
θ	thin	thing	thick	thought	-	-	-	-

B10 Battleships Map 1

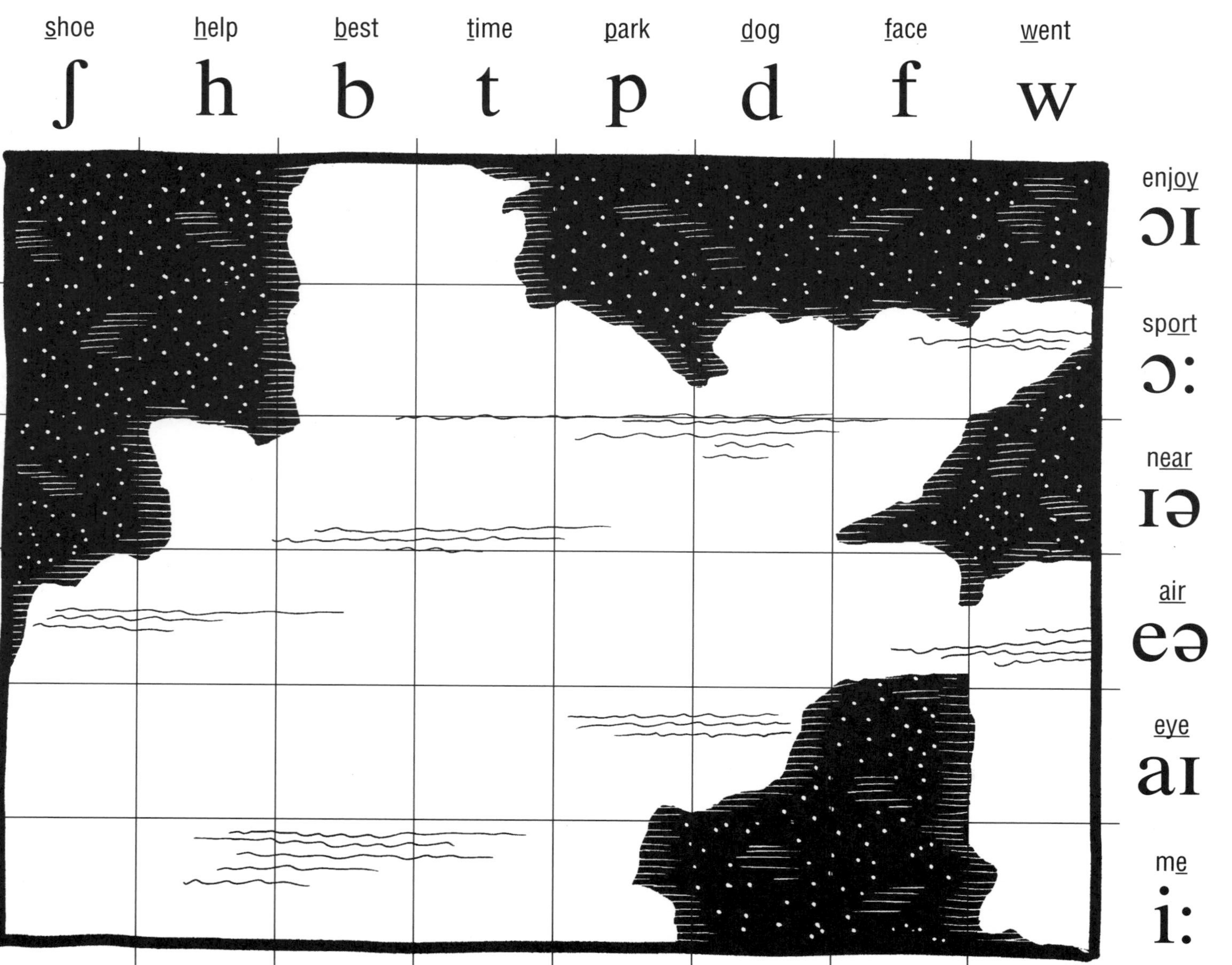

Rules

1 Draw two ships on your map making sure that nobody sees where you have put your ships. You may put your ships inside any square where there is sea (white on the map). Your ships must not cross a line into another square.

2 Work in pairs. The object of the game is to guess where the other player has put the ships and bomb them.

3 To do this, decide which square to bomb and make a word out of the sounds at the side of the map. For example, if the square you want to bomb is in the column with the sound /t/ and the row /i:/, say *tea*.

4 If the square that you bomb contains a ship, the other player must say *hit*. If the square that you bomb is next to a square with a ship in it (including diagonally), the other player must say *near*.

5 Players take turns to bomb each other's ships and the first person to hit both of the other player's ships is the winner.

6 A player whose ship is being bombed may challenge the other player to spell the word that he or she is saying; if the other player is unable to spell the word, he or she misses a turn.

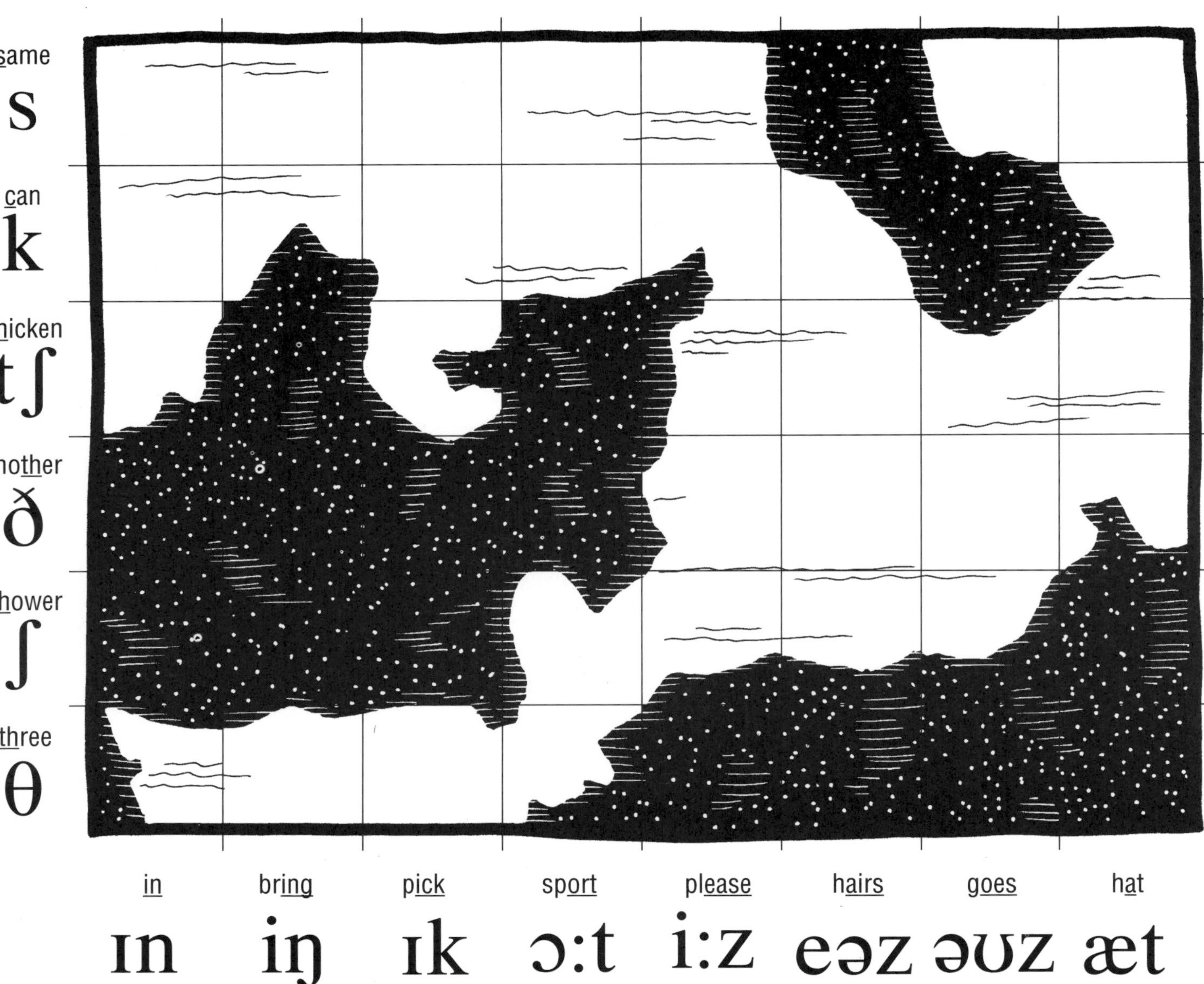

Rules

1 Draw two ships on your map making sure that nobody sees where you have put your ships. You may put your ships inside any square where there is sea (white on the map). Your ships must not cross a line into another square.

2 Work in pairs. The object of the game is to guess where the other player has put the ships and bomb them.

3 To do this, decide which square to bomb and make a word out of the sounds at the side of the map. For example, if the square you want to bomb is in the row with the sound /k/ and the column with the sound /i:z/, say *keys*.

4 If the square that you bomb contains a ship, the other player must say *hit*. If the square that you bomb is next to a square with a ship in it (including diagonally), the other player must say *near*.

5 Players take turns to bomb each other's ships and the first person to hit both of the other player's ships is the winner.

6 A player whose ship is being bombed may challenge the other player to spell the word that he or she is saying; if the other player is unable to spell the word, he or she misses a turn.

Join the dots

B

Point: words and phonetic transcriptions
Minimum level: pre-intermediate
Game type: a matching puzzle for students working individually (or in pairs)
Approximate time: 15 minutes

Preparation

Make a copy of the puzzle for each member of the class. You may also want to make a copy on an OHP transparency or a large piece of paper. There are two puzzles.

Conducting the game

1 Give each student a puzzle. (The puzzle could also be done in pairs.) Explain that to reveal the picture, the dots must be joined in the order shown by the words in the list. To do this, students will need to match words and phonetic transcriptions. Leave students to join the dots.
2 When students have finished, check answers together. (Use your OHP transparency or large piece of paper if you have copied the puzzle.)
3 Drill the pronunciation of the words.

Key

Puzzle 1

Puzzle 2

Puzzle 1

To find out what the cat is doing, match the phonetic transcriptions to words in the picture. Then join the dots by these words in the same order as the list of phonetic transcriptions. Some dots may be used twice.

1 /bəʊn/
2 /bɔ:/
3 /jʌŋ/
4 /beə/
5 /beɪ
6 /ju:z/
7 /jʌŋ/
8 /bɪə/
9 /jɔ:/
10 /bi:/
11 /beɪ/

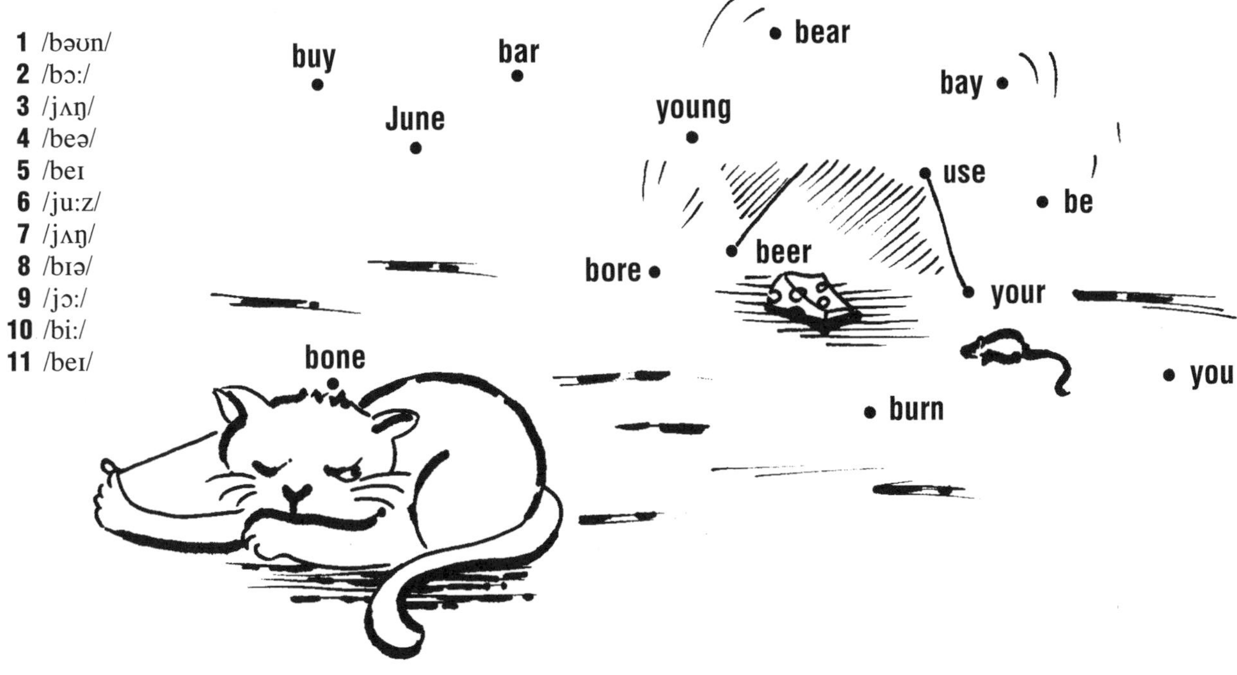

Puzzle 2

To find out what the bear is doing, match the phonetic transcriptions to words in the picture. Then join the dots by these words in the same order as the list of phonetic transcriptions. Some dots may be used twice.

1 /θɪnk/
2 /θri:/
3 /bəʊθ/
4 /waɪn/
5 /wen/
6 /θri:/
7 /ʃu:/
8 /wɒʃ/
9 /peidʒ/
10 /pleɪs/

Phonetic crossword

B

Point: words and phonetic transcriptions
Minimum level: intermediate
Game type: a word puzzle for students working individually (or in pairs)
Approximate time: 15 minutes

Preparation

Make a copy of the puzzle for each member of the class. You may also want to make a copy on an OHP transparency or a large piece of paper. There are two puzzles.

Conducting the game

1 Give each student a word puzzle. (The puzzle could also be done in pairs.) Leave students to complete the puzzle.
2 When students have finished, check answers together. (Use your OHP transparency or large piece of paper if you have copied the puzzle.)
3 Drill the pronunciation of the words.

Key

The completed crosswords should look like this:

Crossword 1

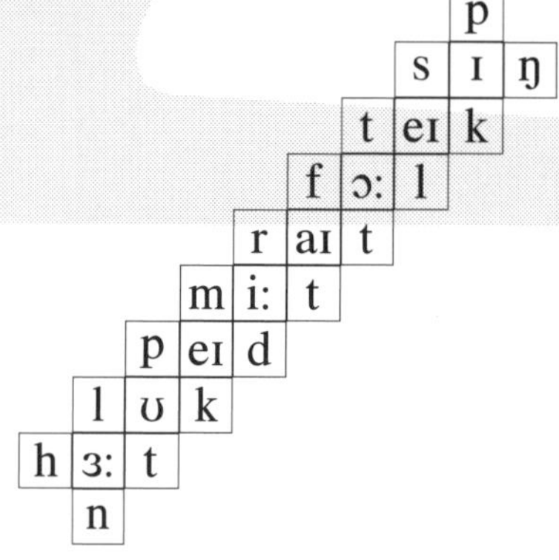

Crossword 2

				s	w
				p	eə
			l	i:	v
h	b	r	eɪ	k	s
ɜ:	r	i:	tʃ	s	i:
d	e	d	i:	s	t
	d	iə	p	i:	

Crossword 1

Complete this crossword with phonetic spellings of these verbs. Use the symbols from the sounds menu. Two of the verbs have been written for you.

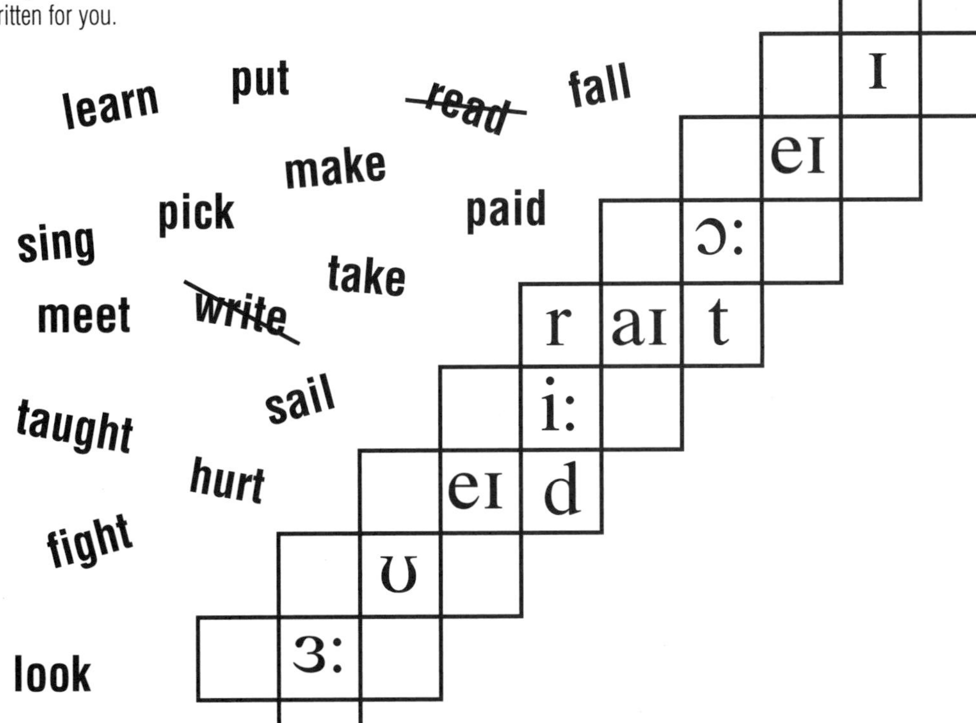

Sounds menu

/p/ park
/f/ face
/t/ time
/d/ dog
/s/ see
/k/ drink
/m/ most
/n/ name
/ŋ/ bring
/h/ here
/l/ live
/r/ ride
/ɪ/ sit
/iː/ seat
/ɔː/ sport
/ɜː/ bird
/ʊ/ good
/eɪ/ face
/aɪ/ line

Crossword 2

Complete this crossword with phonetic symbols from the sounds menu. When it is finished you will see that 'ea' can be pronounced in many different ways.

Across	Down
a **pear**	1 **heard**
b **leave**	2 **bread**
c **break**	3 **read**
d **reach**	4 **cheap**
e **dead**	5 **speaks**
f **east**	6 **sea**
g **dear**	7 **wear**
h **pea**	8 **seat**

Sounds menu

/p/ pen
/b/ bed
/v every
/t/ teach
/d/ dog
/tʃ/ church
/s/ soon
/k/ keep
/h/ hat
/l/ live
/r/ run
/w/ west
/e/ egg
/iː/ see
/ɜː/ bird
/iə/ here
/eə/ hair
/eɪ/ say

13 Sound dice

B

Point: sounds and phonetic symbols
Minimum level: pre-intermediate
Game type: a dice game for two players
Approximate time: 10 minutes

Rules

1 Play this game in pairs, one player with a consonant dice and the other with a vowel dice.

2 Players throw their dice and take turns to try and make a word from the combination of the two sounds on top of the two dice. Throw the dice again if somebody has already made a word from this combination.

3 If a player is unable to find a word, the other player gets a point.

4 The first player to get ten points is the winner.

5 Players may challenge each other to spell a word or give its meaning at any time. If the player who is challenged is unable to do so, the word is not accepted.

Preparation

Provide a set of two dice for each pair of students in the class. Each set of dice consists of a consonant dice and a vowel dice. To make these sets of dice, make or get some cubes (perhaps ordinary dice with the numbers covered by sticky labels) and write the following phonetic symbols on the sides:

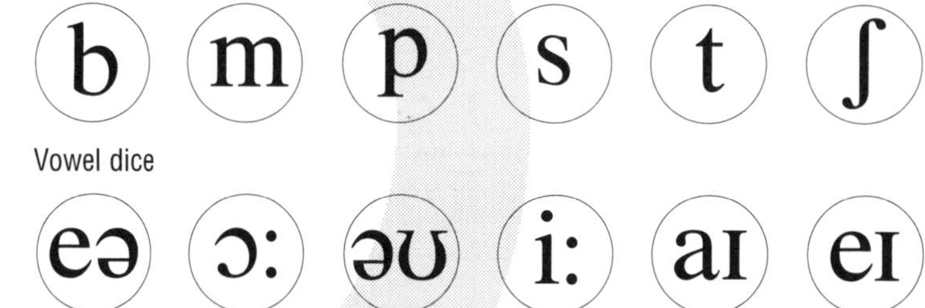

(Note that /eɪ/and /p/ are also /ɪə/ and /d/ respectively when upside down.)
You may also want to make a copy of the rules for each pair of students.

Conducting the game

1 Write the symbols on the board with an example of each for students to refer to during the game.
2 Divide the class into pairs and give each pair a set of dice.
3 Explain the rules.

Key

	/b/	/m/	/p/	/s/	/t/	/ʃ/	/d/
/eə/	bear/bare	mare	pair/pear	-	tear	share	dare
/ɔ:/	bore	more	pour	saw	tore	shore	door
/əʊ/	bow	mow	-	sew/so	toe	show	dough
/i:/	be/bee	me	pea	see	tea	she	-
/aɪ/	buy/by	I'm/my	pie	ice/sigh	tie	shy	die
/eɪ/	bay	may	ape/pay	ace/say	ate	-	day
/ɪə/	beer	mere	peer/pier	-	tear/tier	shear/sheer	dear

Find the rule

B

Point: awareness of sounds
Minimum level: elementary
Game type: a guessing game for the whole class
Approximate time: 10 minutes

Preparation

1 In this game you will need to decide on a rule for accepting or rejecting words suggested by students; they will then try to discover what this rule is.
2 Choose a rule and make a list of words that exemplify this rule. Make sure that your words are from the same grammatical category, eg nouns, and decide upon a model sentence into which your examples will fit, eg *I'm going to buy a ... .*
3 Here are some possible 'rules' and words that exemplify them:

The word must contain two consonant sounds, eg *hat, lock, apple, coat.*
The word must contain only one vowel sound, eg *light, car, house, pea.*
The word must contain three syllables, eg *telephone, magazine, cigarette, elephant.*
The word must end with a consonant sound, eg *light, magazine, lock, house.*

Conducting the game

1 Get the class to sit in more or less a circle.
2 Say your model sentence with an example word in the space. Indicate that the person next to you should repeat the model sentence, changing the word at the end, and so on around the circle. Take part in the game and say a word when it is your turn.
3 After each contribution, say whether or not you accept the word given at the end, but do not say why; students should try to guess this. If your rule is, for example, that the word must contain two consonant sounds, accept any contribution that contains two consonant sounds and do not accept any other.
4 When students catch on to what the rule is, they should not say the rule. Instead, they should simply supply a correct contribution when it is their turn.
5 When most students appear to have caught on, ask someone to explain what the rule is.
6 If nobody seems to be catching on, give a few hints such as *Think about consonant sounds!* The first time you use this game, more hints will probably be necessary.

Bingo

B

Point: discrimination of sounds
Minimum level: elementary
Game type: a listen and search game for the whole class
Approximate time: 20 minutes

Preparation

Copy and cut the sheet of cards so that there is one card for each student. There are cards for two games. The second version of the game consists of two sheets.

Conducting the game

1 Give out the prepared cards.
2 Read out each of the words, from one of the cards in random order. Tick off the words as you read them so as to avoid reading them twice. Ask students to cross out the words on their card as they hear them.
3 When a player completes a horizontal or vertical line on the card, he or she should shout *Bingo!* Ask this player to read back the words in the line that they have completed to see if these words are among the ones you have already read out. This player is the winner.
4 When one player has won, continue the game to give other players an opportunity to reach second and third positions.

Making your own version

1 Make a list of either 16 or 25 words from your course. Make sure that you include plenty of minimal pairs, ie words that are pronounced the same as each other except for one sound.
2 Ask students to draw a grid of squares, either 4 x 4 or 5 x 5.
3 Read out the words on your list and ask students to write the words in the grid in random order. They should ask for the spelling at this stage if they are unsure.
4 Play the game as above.

BINGO 1

bad	boot	pet	beat
part	bed	fat	paid
food	feet	boat	bird
bit	but	fit	put

BINGO 4

pet	beat	boot	part
paid	boat	fat	bad
put	bed	feet	bit
bird	but	fit	food

BINGO 2

bit	food	part	bad
but	feet	bed	boot
bird	boat	fat	pet
fit	paid	put	beat

BINGO 5

part	bad	bit	food
pet	fat	but	feet
boot	boat	bed	bird
beat	paid	put	fit

BINGO 3

beat	paid	pet	boot
bed	put	part	feet
boat	bird	bad	fat
bit	fit	food	but

BINGO 6

fat	paid	beat	pet
boot	put	bad	bed
food	bird	part	fit
feet	but	bit	boat

B15 Bingo Game 2 Sheet 1

BINGO 1

fought	feet	chin	sick	taught
chick	she	share	cheat	thin
seat	short	tea	sort	fee
thought	fair	sin	chair	fin
tin	thick	see	tick	sheet

BINGO 2

taught	thin	fee	fin	sheet
sick	cheat	chin	share	sort
tea	chair	sin	tick	she
feet	fought	see	chick	short
seat	fair	thought	thick	tin

BINGO 3

sheet	tick	fin	see	chair
fee	thick	sin	sort	thin
tin	fair	tea	cheat	taught
thought	short	share	sick	seat
she	chin	chick	feet	fought

BINGO 4

sheet	tick	see	sin	chair
fin	thick	fair	tin	thought
fee	thin	taught	sort	cheat
sick	tea	share	chin	short
she	feet	seat	chick	fought

BINGO 5

she	share	cheat	sort	chair
sin	fair	short	tea	fought
feet	chin	sick	taught	chick
seat	thought	tin	thick	see
tick	sheet	fin	fee	thin

BINGO 6

tin	thick	thought	seat	chick
fought	feet	see	tick	sheet
fin	fee	thin	taught	sick
fair	chin	she	share	cheat
short	sin	tea	chair	sort

Phonetic code

B

Point: awareness of sounds
Minimum level: intermediate
Game type: a search puzzle for students working individually (or in pairs)
Approximate time: 15 minutes

Preparation

Make a copy of the puzzle for each member of the class. You may also want to copy the puzzle onto the board or an OHP transparency.

Presentation

Write on the board:

juice	rain	page
1	2	1, 2

Explain that the numbers refer to sounds; 1 refers to a sound which is common to *juice* and *page* and 2 refers to a sound which is common to *rain* and *page.* Ask students to identify those sounds (1 = the first consonant in *juice,* 2 = the vowel sound in *rain*). If students are familiar with phonetic script, they could use the symbols (1 = /dʒ/, 2 = /eɪ/).

Conducting the game

1 Explain that the three fragments of writing in the puzzle contain a secret message from one spy to another. To find the message, students must break the code.
2 The code is based on the sounds in the words; each number refers to a sound in the word above. If a number occurs under one word and no other, it means that the sound occurs in that word and no other.
3 By putting the sounds that the numbers refer to together in numerical order, you get the secret message. If students are familiar with phonetic script, this will be useful since they will be able to write a symbol for each number.
4 Leave the class to complete the puzzle, giving clues for students who are struggling.

Key

1 meet you (1 = /m/, 2 = /iː/, 3 = /t/, 4 = /j/, 5 = /uː/)

2 airport (1 = /eə/, 2 = /p/, 3 = /ɔː/, 4 = /t/)

3 five thirty (1 = /f/, 2 = /aɪ/, 3 = /v/, 4 = /θ/, 5 = /ɜː/, 6 = /t/, 7 = /ɪ/)

Phonetic code B16

These three sentences contain a secret message from one spy to another. To find the message, you must break the code.

Each of the numbers refers to a sound in the word above it. Put these sounds together in numerical order to find the message.

1 The night is young but soon the yellow moon will rise in the East.

night (3) · young (4) · but (3) · soon (5) · yellow (4) · moon (1 5) · East (2 3)

2 YOU OUGHT TO TASTE THE AIR IN PARIS AND PRAGUE.

OUGHT (3 4) · TO (4) · TASTE (4) · AIR (1) · PARIS (2) · PRAGUE (2)

3 The early bird will never find any worms in the earth before it learns to fly.

early (5) · bird (5) · will (7) · never (3) · find (1 2) · any (7) · worms (5) · in (7) · earth (4 5) · before (1 7) · it (6 7) · learns (5) · to (6) · fly (1 2)

Link maze

C

Point: linking between vowel sounds
Minimum level: intermediate
Game type: a path-finding puzzle for students working individually (or in pairs)
Approximate time: 20 minutes

Preparation

Make a copy of the maze for each member of the class.

Presentation

1 Write the following phrases on the board:

Try again! Two apples Four oranges

Demonstrate the pronunciation of these three phrases, making sure that the words are linked together. Point out that the *y* in *try*, the *w* in *two* and the *r* in *four* are pronounced, whereas they are not when those words are pronounced separately. (Note that the *r* in *four* is pronounced in some accents.)

2 Explain that this is because the second word begins with a vowel, not because of the written *y*, *w* or *r*.

3 Write the following phrases on the board to show how these three sounds can intrude between words even where they are not written:

Three apples Blue eyes Area office

(Note that some people regard the intrusive *r* as in *area office* as bad pronunciation.)

Conducting the game

1 Give each student a maze. (The game could also be played in pairs.) Explain that the object of the game is to find the correct way out of the maze; the exit is from one of the outside squares of the maze.

2 Each square contains a phrase with a linking sound indicated ‿.

3 Players move from square to square according to the following rule:

If the linking sound is /j/, turn left.
If the linking sound is /w/, go straight on.
If the linking sound is /r/, turn right.

It is very important to note that these directions are relative to the side that you enter the square from! So, for example, if you are heading 'east' and turn right, then you will be heading 'south'.

4 When students have finished, check the answers together.

Key

The correct route is as follows:

Hello everybody! - Draw a line - We saw a film - I agree - Where are you? - Blue eyes - Go to England - Law and order - A few apples - Four and a half - Give me a ring - Answer a question - True or false? - Tea or coffee? - We aren't ready - Go ahead! - Score a goal (exit Q)

Making your own versions

You could make your own version using phrases from your course. Simply write the phrases in the squares, then go through the maze yourself to see where players should come out if they move correctly.

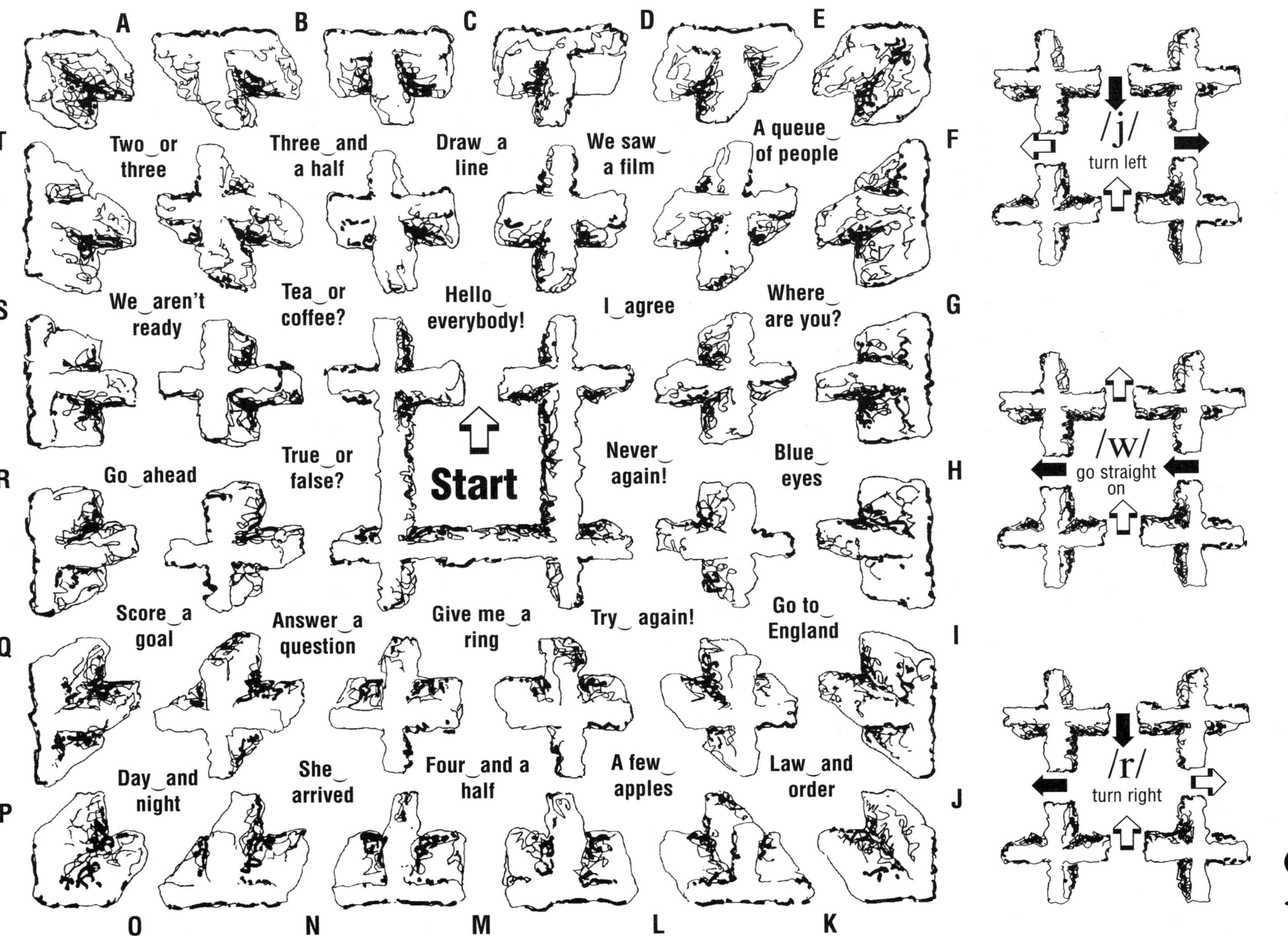
A
B
C
D
E
T
Two_or three
Three_and a half
Draw_a line
We saw_a film
A queue_of people
F
S
We_aren't ready
Tea_or coffee?
Hello_everybody!
I_agree
Where_are you?
G
R
Go_ahead
True_or false?
Start
Never_again!
Blue_eyes
H
Q
Score_a goal
Answer_a question
Give me_a ring
Try_again!
Go to_England
I
P
Day_and night
She_arrived
Four_and a half
A few_apples
Law_and order
J
O
N
M
L
K
/j/
turn left
/w/
go straight on
/r/
turn right

Dictation computer

C2

Point: weak forms (puzzle 1); assimilation (puzzle 2)
Minimum level: intermediate
Game type: a look and find puzzle for students working individually (or in pairs)
Approximate time: 25 minutes

Preparation

Make a copy of the puzzle for each member of the class.

Presentation

1 Write the following phrases on the board. Ask students to pay special attention to the words that are written in small letters as you read out each phrase in turn. Make sure that you use the weak form of each word that is written in small letters.

WHAT'S her NAME? /ˈwɒts ə ˈneɪm/
WHAT'S your NUMBER? /ˈwɒts jə ˈnʌmbə/
JOHN can SWIM /ˈdʒɒn kən ˈswɪm/
TEA for TWO /ˈtiː fə ˈtuː/
the PRICE has FALLEN /ðə ˈpraɪs əz ˈfɔːlən/
FISH and CHIPS /ˈfɪʃ ən ˈtʃɪps/
GO to BED /ˈgəʊ tə ˈbed/
DOGS are FRIENDLY /ˈdɒgz ə ˈfrendlɪ/
HAVE a DRINK /ˈhæv ə ˈdrɪnk/
WHAT does SARAH DO? /ˈwɒt dəz ˈseərə duː/

2 Elicit or explain that the weak form words are grammatical words rather than items of vocabulary. Ask students to try and pronounce the phrases with the weak forms.

3 Write up the following phrases on the board:

a major decision **b** made your decision

Explain that these could both be pronounced exactly the same when the weak form is used - /ˈmeɪdʒədɪˈsɪʒən/.

4 Naturally, the context would clarify which of the two messages was meant. However, on sound alone, they could not be distinguished. Consequently, if a computer were designed that could write down everything that it heard, it might write *Buying a house is always a made your decision* instead of *Buying a house is always a major decision.*

5 Write the following phrase on the board and explain that it is something the dictation computer wrote that contains a mistake:

Don't lighter your mother!

Ask the class to try to identify the error. As a clue, you could give the reply:

Why not? She always lies to me!

Conducting the game

Give each student a puzzle. (The puzzle could also be done in pairs.) Leave students to find the errors and solve the puzzle.

C2

Dictation computer

Key Puzzle 1

The dictation computer should have written:

1 I'll ask her if ... (c)

2 I compose music ... (e)

3 The officers changed ... (a)

4 Did you see the waiter go ... (b)

5 ... is on the centre page. (d)

6 I picked your book ... (h)

7 Will you ever forgive me? (f)

8 ... shows all the cities and railways ... (j)

9 Spiders are not really insects ... (g)

10 ... are rival companies. (i)

Follow-up

A second version of the puzzle is similar, but focuses on assimilation. Here, the dictation computer makes mistakes like this:

shop people instead of *shot people*
knock quickly instead of *not quickly*
dig carefully instead of *did carefully*

The reason for these mistakes is that the final consonant sound in each of the first words is changed by the initial consonant sound in each of the second words.

Key Puzzle 2

The dictation computer should have written:

1 I don't like green. (c)

2 You should wipe plates ... (a)

3 ... I ran quickly ... (d)

4 We ate quite badly ... (e)

5 ... go to the gym ... (b)

6 ... unless I warn my parents ... (f)

7 ... the term before last. (g)

8 This lead covering ... (i)

9 ... the family of the bride ... (j)

10 ... told us to wait quietly ... (h)

C2 Dictation computer **Puzzle 1** (weak forms)

The dictation computer prints exactly what it hears. Sometimes, however, there is more than one possibility and the computer makes a mistake.

Find the errors in the computer's work in the left hand column. Then match the sentences with their responses in the right hand column.

Use the responses as clues if you have difficulty finding the mistakes.

Alaska if she wants to come with us. **1**	**a** <u>Who</u> changed into civilian clothes?
I can pose music for TV programmes. **2**	**b** Yes; I saw him going into the kitchen.
The office has changed into civilian clothes. **3**	**c** You'll ask <u>who</u>?
Did you see the way to go? He was at the next table a minute ago. **4**	**d** Really? It used to be on the back page.
In this newspaper, the TV guide is on the sent a page. **5**	**e** I didn't know you were a composer.
I picture book off the floor. **6**	**f** Only if you promise never to do it again.
Will you ever for give me? **7**	**g** They look like insects to me!
This map shows all the citizen railways in the country. **8**	**h** Oh thanks! I didn't realise I'd dropped it.
Spy does are not really insects you know. **9**	**i** Do you think so? I think they work together, myself.
Coke and Pepsi arrival companies. **10**	**j** It doesn't show the smaller places then?

C2 Dictation computer

(assimilation) **Puzzle 2**

The dictation computer prints exactly what it hears. Sometimes, however, there is more than one possibility and the computer makes a mistake.

Find the errors in the computer's work in the left hand column. Then match the sentences with their responses in the right hand column.

Use the responses as clues if you have difficulty finding the mistakes.

I don't light green. **1**	**a** Yes, but not if you're using them every day.
You should white plates to get the dust off before serving the food. **2**	**b** So that's how you manage to stay so fit!
Being late for work, I rang quickly out of the house. **3**	**c** Well, do you like blue?
We ache quite badly when we were on holiday because we didn't like the local food. **4**	**d** I suppose that's why you forgot to take your keys.
I always go to the gin before work in the morning. **5**	**e** Yes, you seem to have lost weight.
I'm not allowed to have a party unless I warm my parents a week in advance. **6**	**f** I'm glad my parents are more easy going than yours.
I failed my maths exam the turn before last. **7**	**g** Is that why you had to do it again last term?
This leg covering is for protection against radiation. **8**	**h** And I suppose you all made a lot of noise, as usual?
Traditionally, the family of the bribe paid for the wedding. **9**	**i** Well, if they drop the bomb, I'd rather die than have to stay in there!
The teacher told us to wake quietly until the bell rang. **10**	**j** Nowadays, both families tend to split the costs.

Da da language

Point: stress timing
Minimum level: pre-intermediate
Game type: an oral matching game for students working in pairs
Approximate time: 25 minutes

Preparation

Make a copy of the *Da da phrase book* for each member of the class. These may be collected in at the end of the game and used again.

Presentation

1 Explain that you are going to teach the class a new language called *Da da*. This language has three words; *Dar* /da:/, *Dooby* /du:bɪ/ and *Dipety* /dɪpətɪ/. Write up some phrases or sentences in *Da da*, such as:

Dar dooby dar   Dipety dooby dar

Invite students to read the words out.

2 Now explain that you are going to tell the class how to translate *Da da* into English. Give out the copies of the *Da da phrase book*. Explain that the secret to the translation lies in the stress patterns. The stress patterns for the three words *Dar, Dooby* and *Dipety* are ●, ●• and ●•• respectively. Point out that the English words or groups of words in the phrase book also have these three stress patterns. For example, *Fresh* = ●, *Lots of* = ●• and *Plenty of* = ●••.

3 To translate a *Da da* sentence of three words, select the English words or groups of words with the same stress pattern. So, in box 1 for example, *Dar dar dar* would translate as *Fresh fried chips*, and *Dar Dipety Dooby* would translate as *Fresh carrots and pizza.*

4 For each of the boxes 1-8, call out the simple *Da da* sentences *Dar dar dar, Dooby dooby dooby* and *Dipety dipety dipety* and ask students to call out the translation. The drill should begin like this:

T Dar dar dar
Ss Fresh fried chips
T Dooby dooby dooby
Ss Lots of fish and pizza

Make sure that students maintain the same rhythm. The rhythm could be tapped out like this:

tap tap tap - (pause) - tap tap tap - (pause) - etc.

5 Ask individual students to translate more complex sentences such as *Dipety dooby dar.* Say beforehand which of the boxes 1-8 to use.

Conducting the game

1 Divide the class into pairs.
2 Players take turns to formulate sentences for their partner to translate into English.
3 When students are getting used to this procedure, they could begin to play for points; each player starts with ten points and loses a point for each mistake.

Da da phrase book

1	**Dar**	Fresh	fried	chips
	Dooby	Lots of	fish and	pizza
	Dipety	Plenty of	carrots and	sausages
2	**Dar**	New	black	boots
	Dooby	Lovely	yellow	trousers
	Dipety	Horrible	rose coloured	sunglasses
3	**Dar**	Don't	tell	Mike
	Dooby	Go and	speak to	Mary
	Dipety	Hurry and	give it to	Jonathan
4	**Dar**	Near	north	Leeds
	Dooby	There in	sunny	London
	Dipety	Over in	glamorous	Manchester

Da da phrase book

5	**Dar**	One	cold	beer
	Dooby	Half a	glass of	whiskey
	Dipety	Give me a	bottle of	orange juice
6	**Dar**	Ring	Jack	soon
	Dooby	Speak to	Susan	later
	Dipety	Telephone	Alison	afterwards
7	**Dar**	Three	blind	mice
	Dooby	Seven	hungry	tigers
	Dipety	Hundreds of	pictures of	elephants
8	**Dar**	Can't	Pete	drive?
	Dooby	Doesn't	Oscar	listen?
	Dipety	Can't you make	Jennifer	talk to you?

Fishing

C

Point: stress patterns in short phrases
Minimum level: intermediate
Game type: a matching puzzle for students working individually (or in pairs)
Approximate time: 15 minutes

Preparation
Make a copy of the puzzle for each member of the class.

Presentation
1 Choose some short phrases from your course and write them on the board. Read the phrases aloud to demonstrate their stress patterns and draw a circle under the stressed syllables. These stressed syllables will be in the content words as opposed to the grammatical words. Draw a smaller circle under each of the remaining syllables. These syllables will be the unstressed parts of the content words and the form words. (Note that the stress patterns could be different if one part of the message is given a special emphasis for some reason.)
2 Ask students to think of some other phrases and indicate the stress pattern with circles.

Conducting the game
1 Give each student a puzzle. (The puzzle could also be done in pairs.) Explain that for each of the phrases around the edge of the pond, there is another phrase with the same stress pattern elsewhere. The object of the game is to draw straight lines joining these matching pairs of phrases to discover which fish is caught.
2 A fish is caught if it is completely surrounded by lines.
3 One strategy would be to begin by marking the stress patterns under each of the phrases.

Key
Fish B is caught. The correct matching pairs are:

- ● Look! - Wait!
- •● Begin! - She talked.
- ●● Who cares? - Don't stop!
- ●●• Don't worry! - Keep quiet!
- ••● They've arrived.- I insist.
- •●• They've finished. - I've seen it.
- ●•● What's the time? - Don't forget!
- ●•●• See you later! - Come and see us!
- •●•● I spoke to John. - He wants to come.
- ●••● Where was he from? - What do you want?
- •●•●• She tried to call you. - I can't believe it.

Making your own versions
You can make your own version using phrases from your course. Draw the points and join pairs of them up. Choose one enclosed area to place the caught fish. Place the rest of the fish in unenclosed areas. Label all the fish with letters of the alphabet. Trace the points and fish onto a second sheet of paper and write the phrases by the points. Make sure that you have a matching pair by two points that were connected by a line on the first sheet of paper.

Join the dots next to the sentences with matching stress patterns. There is only one pair of sentences for each stress pattern. The eleven stress patterns in the game are:

● •● ●● ●●• ••● •●•

●•● ●•●• •●•● ●••● •●•●•

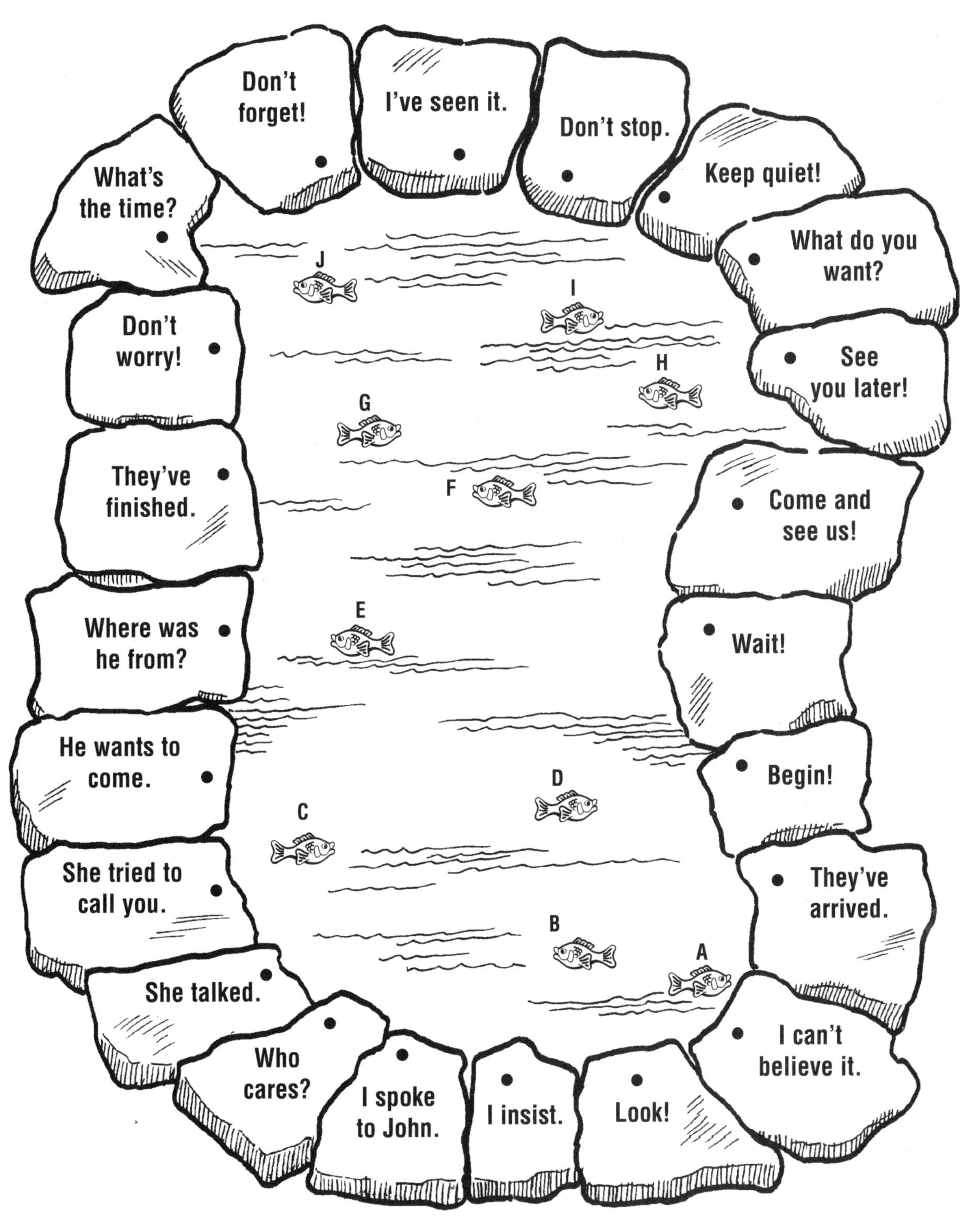

Compound clues

Point: stress patterns in compound nouns
Minimum level: intermediate
Game type: a find-the-difference memory game for students working in pairs
Approximate time: 30 minutes

Preparation

Make copies of the two pictures for each pair of students. You may also want to make copies on OHP transparencies or large pieces of paper.

Presentation

1 Give out copies of the first picture - John Barnet's front room, August 5th, 11 a.m. (Use your OHP transparency or large piece of paper if you have copied the picture.) Ask students to label all the objects in the picture which are compound nouns. This can be made easier by writing the compound nouns on the board (see key) and asking students to identify them in the picture. If you do this, write the compound nouns in two columns according to whether the stress is on the first or second element.
2 Check answers with the class. (Write the words on the board in two columns if you did not do this in stage 1.)
3 Read out words at random from the board and ask students to try and identify the reason for the words being separated into two columns.
4 Explain the rule behind the pattern; the rule is that with compound nouns formed from two simple nouns, the stress is normally on the first element. However, it tends to be on the second element when the first element is:

- **a** the material that the second element is made of, eg *plastic bag.*
- **b** the location of the second element, eg *kitchen sink.*

5 Drill the pronunciation of the compound nouns.

Conducting the game

1 Remove the first picture or ask students to turn it over. Show or give out the second picture.
2 Allow students five minutes to study the picture and identify what has changed.
3 Invite students to report the changes. You could combine this with grammar practice, eg:

present perfect - *Someone has moved the candlestick.*
present perfect passive - *The car radio has been stolen.*

Compound clues

C

Key

1 These are the compound nouns in the pictures. How many you focus upon will depend on the level of your class.

stress on **first** element (both pictures):
birthday card, bookcase, bottle opener, candlestick, coat hanger, hairbrush, hair-dryer, handbag, light switch, newspaper, penknife, suitcase, teapot, table-cloth, toothbrush, vacuum cleaner

stress on **first** element (picture 1 only):
dartboard, door handle

stress on **second** element (both pictures):
cheese sandwich, front door, straw hat, tomato sauce

stress on **second** element (picture 1 only):
car radio, wooden spoon

stress on **second** element (picture 2 only):
kitchen door, kitchen floor, kitchen sink, kitchen window, paper plane

2 These are the differences in the two pictures showing what happened between 11 a.m. and 12 noon:
candlestick moved, car radio gone, cheese sandwich bitten, kitchen door opened, tomato sauce knocked over, wooden spoon gone.The kitchen window is broken in picture 2. There is also a body on the kitchen floor and a paper plane on the living room floor.

Follow-up

1 Ask students in small groups to make up a story to explain the changes between 11 a.m. and 12 noon. There is no set answer to this.
2 Ask the groups to tell their stories to the class, insisting on correct pronunciation of the compound nouns. Or record the stories and ask the class to identify errors when the tape is played back.

C5 Compound clues Picture 1

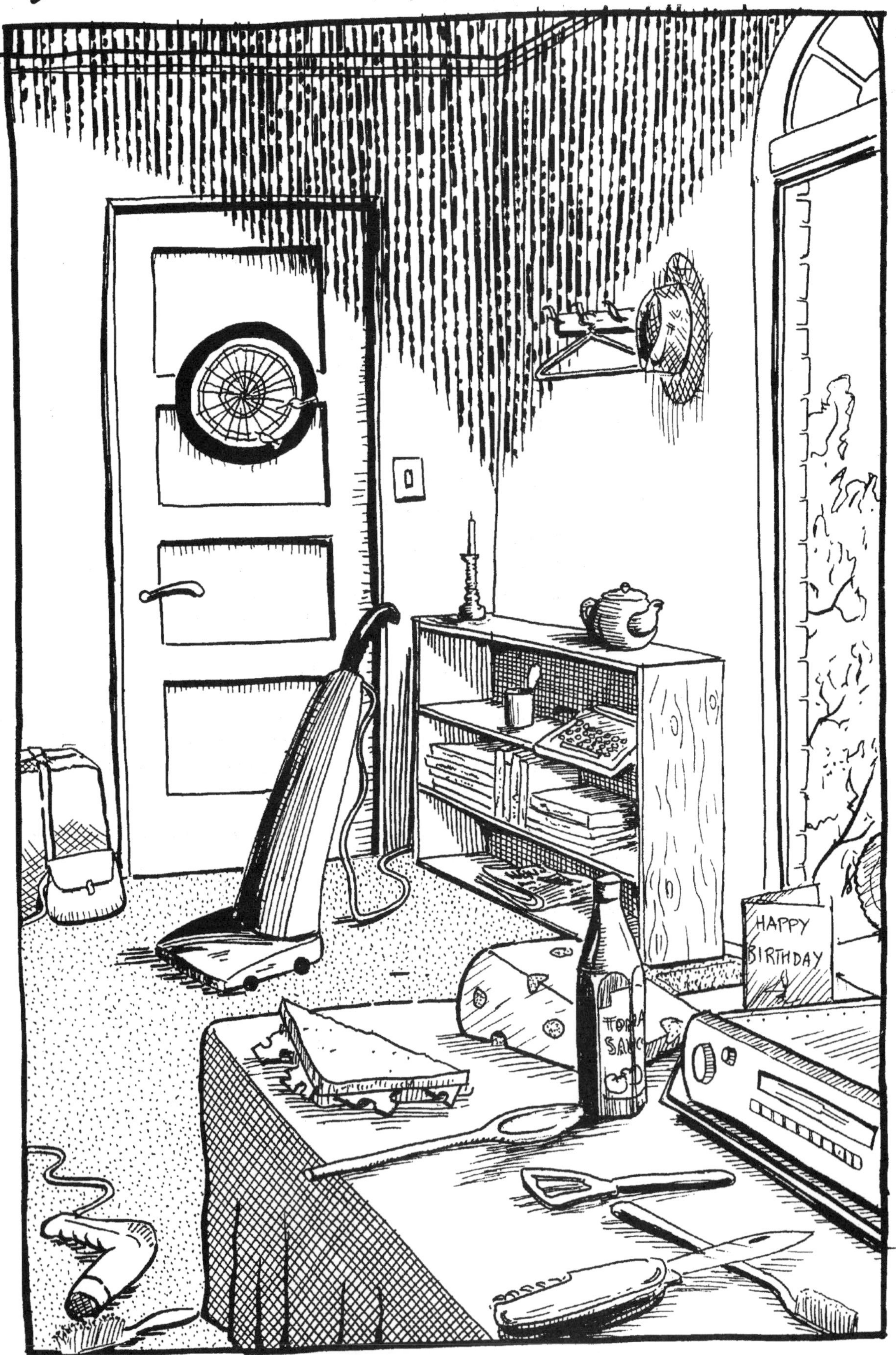

John Barnet's front room **August 5th, 11 a.m.**

John Barnet's front room

August 5th, 12 noon

Rhythm dominoes

C

Point: stress patterns in short phrases
Minimum level: pre-intermediate
Game type: a matching game with cards for three or four players
Approximate time: 25 minutes

Rules

1 Play this game in groups of three or four. Deal the same number of cards to each player. If you are playing in a group of three, place one card in the middle as a starter.

2 Take turns to place cards on the table and build a track. You must place one of your cards so that it touches one of the two end cards in the track. The phrases in the sides that are next to each other must contain the same stress pattern.

3 A player who is unable to place a card when it is his or her turn, misses that turn; a player who places a card incorrectly must take the card back and miss a turn.

4 The first player to place all his or her cards in the track is the winner.

Preparation

Copy and cut out a set of dominoes for each group of three or four students in the class.

Presentation

1 Write on the board a list of the following stress pattern symbols:

1 ●•● 2 •●• 3 ●●• 4 ●•●• 5 •●•● 6 ●••●

Next to pattern 1 write an example, such as *Close the door* and say the phrase aloud to illustrate its stress pattern.

2 On another part of the board, write an example of one of the other patterns, such as *Can't you hear me?* (●•●•) Invite students to identify its stress pattern. As a first step, ask them how many syllables the phrase has; then ask which syllables are stressed. Note that for the sake of simplicity, all the words in the phrases in this game consist of only one syllable.

3 Choose examples of the other patterns from the key, so that finally you have on the board one example for each pattern.

Conducting the game

1 Divide the class into groups of three or four and give each group a set of dominoes.

2 Explain and/or give out the rules.

3 During the game, move around the class helping students to resolve any disputes. Look at the cards that have been played to check that the matching pairs of phrases are correct.

Follow-up

As a follow-up activity, you could try to elicit the rule behind the stress patterns in the game, that is, that 'content' words are stressed and grammatical or 'form' words are unstressed.

Key

1	●•●	Come and look. Yes, of course.	Close the door. Fish and chips.	What's the time? Thanks a lot.
2	•●•	She saw us. I like it.	You've met them. I think so.	He told me.
3	●●•	Who saw them? Please tell me.	Who did it? Don't break it.	John rang us.
4	●•●•	Can't you hear me? Come and see us.	Don't you like it? Try to call me.	Pleased to meet you. Phone and tell me.
5	•●•●	A piece of cake. The shop was closed.	It's time to go. It's cold and wet.	The bus is late.
6	●••●	Where do you live? Give me a call.	How do you do? What was his name?	Where are you from?

Rules

1 Play this game in groups of three or four. Deal the same number of cards to each player. If you are playing in a group of three, place one card in the middle as a starter.

2 Take turns to place cards on the table and build a track. You must place one of your cards so that it touches one of the two end cards in the track. The phrases in the sides that are next to each other must contain the same stress pattern.

3 A player who is unable to place a card when it is his or her turn, misses that turn; a player who places a card incorrectly must take the card back and miss a turn.

4 The first player to place all his or her cards in the track is the winner.

Close the door.
It's time to go.
She saw us.
How do you do?
Where do you live?
A piece of cake.
Can't you hear me?
You've met them.
Who did it?
What's the time?
The bus is late.
John rang us.

C6 Rhythm dominoes Sheet 2

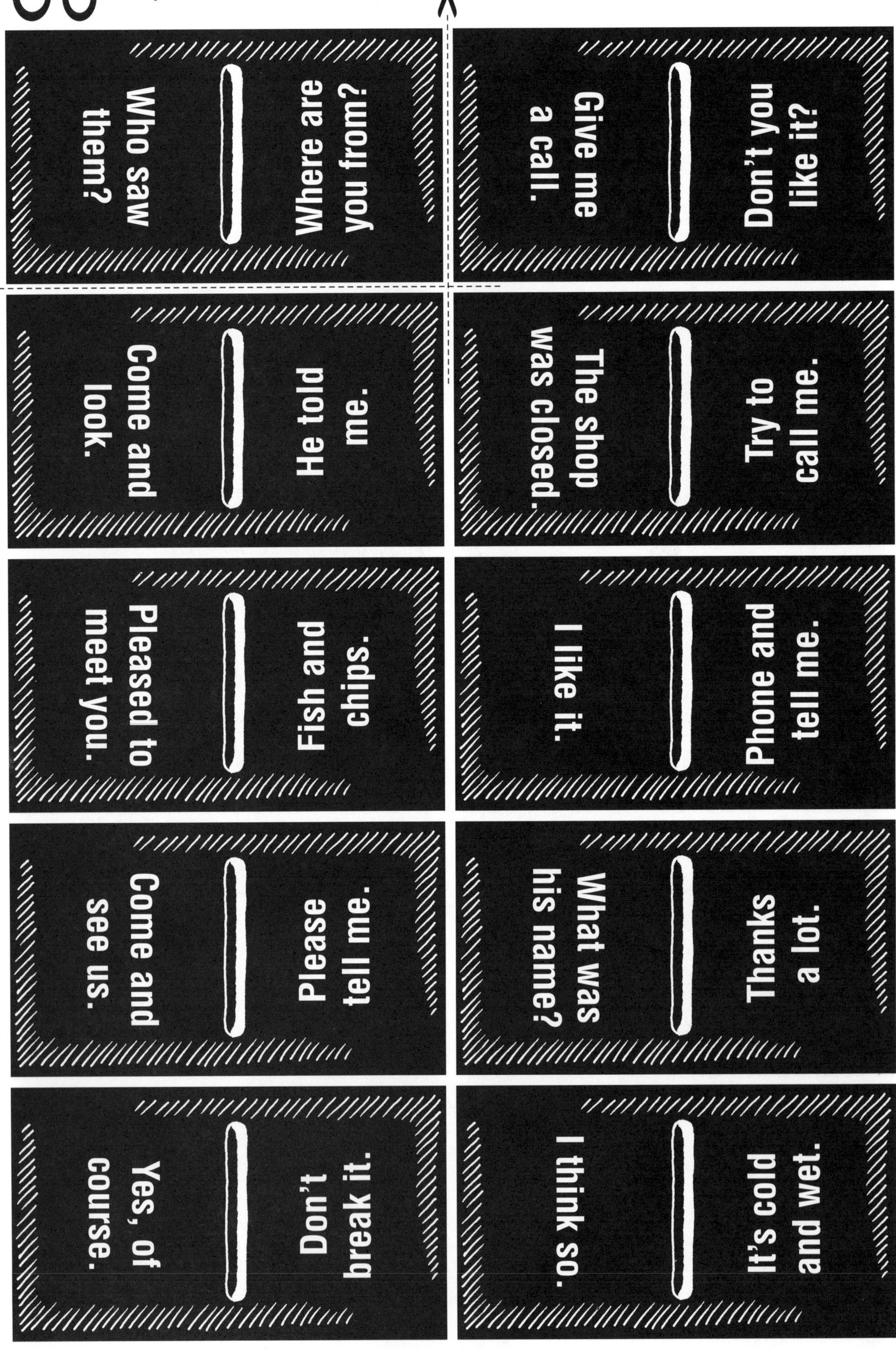

Who saw them?
Where are you from?
Give me a call.
Don't you like it?
Come and look.
He told me.
The shop was closed.
Try to call me.
Pleased to meet you.
Fish and chips.
I like it.
Phone and tell me.
Come and see us.
Please tell me.
What was his name?
Thanks a lot.
Yes, of course.
Don't break it.
I think so.
It's cold and wet.

Contradict me

Point: contrastive stress
Minimum level: intermediate
Game type: a card game quiz for three or four players
Approximate time: 25 minutes

Rules

1 The aim of the game is to win as many cards as possible.

2 Place the pack of cards face down on the table.

3 Take turns to pick up a card and read the sentence at the top of the card to the player sitting on your right. (The sentence at the bottom shows the mistake.)

4 This player must reply by correcting the mistake and using contrastive stress. The reply should begin with a phrase such as *You mean ...?, I thought ...?, Don't you mean ...?*

5 The reader should say if the response was correct or not. The other players should also help to decide.

6 If the response is correct, the player who gave the response wins the card. Otherwise, the reader keeps the card.

Preparation

Copy and cut out a set of cards for each group of three or four students in the class.

Presentation

1 Write on the board the following two sentences and invite students to correct the mistakes:

My mother's name is John.

The formula for water is H_3O.

2 Write up the following sentences as possible responses:

You mean your <u>father's</u> name is John!

I thought the formula for water was $H_{\underline{2}}O$.

Read out the pairs of sentences to demonstrate the contrastive stress on *father's* and *2*. Drill the sentences as mini-dialogues. Provide some more ways of beginning the response, eg *Surely you mean ...?, Don't you mean ...?* and *Oh? I was told ... .*

3 Say a few more contentious sentences, perhaps from the game, and invite students to correct the mistakes. Remind them to change the pronoun, as in the example *My mother's name* above where *my* is changed to *your* in the response.

Conducting the game

1 Divide the class into groups of three or four and give each group a set of cards.

2 Explain and/or give out the rules.

3 During the game move around the class helping to resolve any disputes. (Note that responses other than those on the cards are possible.)

Follow-up

Students make up their own statements with mistakes for their classmates to correct.

…uict me Sheet 1

Rules

1 The aim of the game is to win as many cards as possible.

2 Place the pack of cards face down on the table.

3 Take turns to pick up a card and read the sentence at the top of the card to the player sitting on your right. (The sentence at the bottom shows the mistake.)

4 This player must reply by correcting the mistake and using contrastive stress. The reply should begin with a phrase such as *You mean ...?*, *I thought ...?*, *Don't you mean ...?*

5 The reader should say if the response was correct or not. The other players should also help to decide.

6 If the response is correct, the player who gave the response wins the card. Otherwise, the reader keeps the card.

My mother's name is John.	**The capital of France is London.**	**I had dinner at 8.30 this morning.**	**Robert de Niro is a well known actress.**
... your <u>father's</u> name is John!	... the capital of <u>Britain</u> is London / the capital of France is <u>Paris</u>!	... you had <u>breakfast</u> at 8.30 this morning / you had dinner at 8.30 this <u>evening</u>!	... Robert de Niro is a well known <u>actor</u>!
Brazil is the biggest country in North America.	**The Greeks built the pyramids.**	**My sister is a policeman.**	**The Atlantic is the world's biggest ocean.**
... Brazil is the biggest country in <u>South</u> America / <u>Canada</u> is the biggest country in North America!	... the <u>Egyptians</u> built the pyramids!	... your sister is a <u>policewoman</u> / your <u>brother</u> is a policeman!	... the <u>Pacific</u> is the world's biggest ocean!
I saw the news on the radio.	**It was hot so I put my coat on.**	**I'd like a piece of cola please.**	**The lion is in the dog family.**
... You <u>heard</u> the news on the radio / you saw the news on the <u>TV</u>!	... it was <u>cold</u> so you put your coat on / it was hot so you took your coat <u>off</u>!	... you'd like a <u>cup/glass</u> of cola!	... the lion is in the <u>cat</u> family / the <u>wolf</u> is in the dog family!

The sun sets in the morning.	**I like to smoke a gin and tonic in the evening.**	**The elephant is the biggest animal in the sea.**	**Have you read the latest film?**	**The Nile is the world's shortest river.**	**These gloves are too small; they hurt my feet.**
... the sun <u>rises</u> in the morning / the sun sets in the <u>evening</u>!	... you like to <u>drink</u> a gin and tonic in the evening / you like to smoke a <u>cigarette</u> in the evening!	... the elephant is the biggest animal on the <u>land</u> / the <u>whale</u> is the biggest animal in the sea!	... have I <u>seen</u> the latest film / read the latest <u>book</u>!	... the Nile is the world's <u>longest</u> river!	... these <u>socks/shoes</u> are too small; they hurt your feet / these gloves are too small; they hurt your <u>hands</u>!
Everest is the lowest mountain in the world.	**Beethoven became blind near the end of his life.**	**Cleopatra lived in Australia.**	**Pele was a great Argentinian footballer.**	**New Delhi is the capital of Kenya.**	**Gold is a very cheap metal.**
... Everest is the <u>highest</u> mountain in the world!	... Beethoven became <u>deaf</u> near the end of his life!	... Cleopatra lived in <u>Africa</u>!	... Pele was a great <u>Brazilian</u> footballer!	... New Delhi is the capital of <u>India</u> / <u>Nairobi</u> is the capital of Kenya!	... gold is a very <u>expensive</u> metal!
Kangaroos come from Austria.	**Carrots are my favourite fruit.**	**There were five people in the Beatles.**	**Two plus two equals five.**	**The formula for water is H_3O.**	**I fell upstairs and broke my leg.**
... kangaroos come from <u>Australia</u>!	... carrots are your favourite <u>vegetable</u>!	... there were <u>four</u> people in the Beatles!	... two plus two equals <u>four</u> / two plus <u>three</u> equals five!	... the formula for water is $H_{\underline{2}}O$!	... you fell <u>downstairs</u> and broke your leg!

Don't tell me

Point: intonation for shared and new information
Minimum level: intermediate
Game type: a guessing game for two players
Approximate time: 30 minutes

Rules

1 The object of the game is to win as many cards as possible.

2 Play the game in pairs. Take turns to be speaker and listener.

3 The speaker takes a card from the pack and reads the questions.

4 The listener should respond by saying *Yes* after each question.

5 If the listener can guess the end of the speaker's story after the speaker has made six statements, he or she can say *Don't tell me ...* and give the end of the story. If it is correct, the listener wins the card. If it is incorrect, the speaker reads the end of the story from the card.

6 If the speaker reads the end of the story, he or she wins the card. At the end of the story, the listener must make an appropriate exclamation such as *How terrible!* or *How wonderful!*

Preparation

Copy and cut out a set of cards for each pair of students in the class.

Presentation

1 Write the following dialogue on the board or OHP (without the intonation marked to begin with):

A You know John?
B Yes.
A Well, you know the street where he lives?
B Yes.
A Well, you know that big house at the end?
B Yes.
A You remember it was for sale?
B Yes.
A And I said I was thinking of buying it?
B Yes.
A Well, I have!
B Oh, how fantastic!

This dialogue is an exaggerated example of a style of speaking in which speaker A tries to build up suspense before giving some news. It demonstrates that intonation tends to fall-rise on old or shared information and fall on new information. The rise-fall on the final exclamation is also typical of exclamations; it indicates emotions such as surprise and disgust.

2 Concentrate first on *Yes*. Model saying it with a falling intonation and then with a fall-rise intonation and ask students to mimic you. Indicate that they should use the fall-rise version in the dialogue.

3 Focus on the exclamation *Oh, how fantastic!* and model the rise-fall intonation. Ask students to mimic you.

4 Now read through the whole dialogue with the class. Take part A yourself. Draw attention to the fall-rise on A's questions and draw the arrows onto the dialogue.

5 Ask various students to read part A and the rest of the class to read part B.

6 Introduce as an alternative response for B after A's fifth question. *Don't tell me; you've bought it!* then A would respond something like *Yes, that's right. How did you know?* Drill the dialogue again using this version.

Conducting the game

1 Divide the class into pairs and give each pair a pack of cards. Make one group of three if there is an odd number of students in the class. Ask these students to take turns reading and responding.

2 Explain and/or give out the rules.

3 During the game, move around the class helping students to resolve any disputes. This will be especially necessary in deciding whether a player's guess is close enough to the right answer.

Don't tell me C8

Rules

1 The object of the game is to win as many cards as possible.

2 Play the game in pairs. Take turns to be speaker and listener.

3 The speaker takes a card from the pack and reads the questions.

4 The listener should respond by saying *Yes* after each question.

5 If the listener can guess the end of the speaker's story after the speaker has made six statements, he or she can say *Don't tell me ...* and give the end of the story. If it is correct, the listener wins the card. If it is incorrect, the speaker reads the end of the story from the card.

6 If the speaker reads the end of the story, he or she wins the card. At the end of the story, the listener must make an appropriate exclamation such as *How terrible!* or *How wonderful!*

- You know my sister's boyfriend Tim?
- Well, you know he's in my class?
- And you know he always gets the best grades?
- And you know that's why my sister likes him?
- Well, you know we got our reports back last week?
- And his was terrible?
- **Well, my sister is leaving him!**

- You know that new film that's on, 'Spartans'?
- And you know it was filmed in Greece?
- And you know I was in Greece on holiday last year?
- And you remember that part where a lion escapes?
- And all the crowd runs out of the theatre?
- And you know they sometimes get ordinary people to be in crowds in films?
- **Well, I was in that crowd!**

- You know the group 'The Lead Feathers'?
- Well, you know they've got a great drummer?
- You know his name's Stix Morton?
- Well, you know he lives near here?
- And you know I'm learning the drums?
- And you know I saw Stix in the pub last week?
- **Well, he's agreed to give me lessons!**

- You remember Mike?
- Well, you know he's always talking about motorbikes?
- And you know he bought one last year?
- And you know he crashed it last month?
- And you know he said he wasn't going to buy one ever again?
- And you know he was saving to buy a car instead?
- **Well, he's just bought a new motorbike!**

- You remember Sally?
- Well, you know her friend Lynne?
- You remember Lynne broke her leg?
- And of course you know my brother is a doctor?
- And you know he fixed her leg?
- And you know they started going out together?
- **Well, they're getting married!**

- You know my new car?
- Well, you know it had a tape recorder in it?
- You remember it didn't work properly?
- And I took it back to the shop?
- And I had to wait two months to get a new one?
- And you know it arrived last week?
- **Well, it was stolen yesterday!**

Intonation monopoly

C

Point: intonation in question tags
Minimum level: upper intermediate
Game type: a racing game with board and cards for three or four players
Approximate time: 30 minutes

Rules

1 Place the cards face down in the middle of the board and the counters on the square marked *Start*. Players move around the board. Each time a player passes *Start* he or she may write his or her name on any square on the board; no other player can then land on that square. The first player to pass *Start* three times is the winner.

2 Players take turns to pick up a card and move.

3 When a player picks up a card, he or she must read the sentence on it and complete it with a tag question with the appropriate intonation. If the intonation is correct, the player can then move to the next square with that tag question and that intonation (as marked by the arrow).

4 If a player arrives at a square which is the start of an arrow pointing forwards, he or she can move to the square indicated if he or she can suggest a sentence that would naturally lead to that tag question.

5 If a player arrives at a square which is the start of an arrow pointing backwards, the player must move to the square indicated unless he or she can suggest a sentence that would naturally lead to that tag question.

6 If a player lands on a square with another player's name in it, the player must return to the square he or she came from.

Preparation

Copy a board and set of cards for each group of three or four students in the class. Cut out the cards. Provide a counter for each student.

Presentation

The game assumes that students have already looked at question tags and know that the tag should agree with the main verb and that normally the tag is negative if the main verb is positive and vice versa.

1 Write on the board the following sentences (without the intonation marked):

A: How's your headache? It isn't getting worse, is↗it?

B: It's not very nice weather, is↘it?

2 Model the sentences, being careful to use a rising intonation on the tag in sentence A and a falling intonation on the tag in sentence B. Ask students to listen and identify the difference in the intonation of the tag in the two sentences.

3 Explain that one of the questions is real since the speaker does not know the answer. The other sentence is not really a question, since the speaker knows the answer and is only asking for confirmation. Ask students to identify which is which. (A is the real question.) Explain that the difference in intonation in the tag questions signals whether or not the question is real.

4 Draw the intonation patterns onto the sentences on the board, rising for A (*is↗it?*) and falling for B (*is↘it?*). Read the tag only from A or B and ask students to identify which one you are saying; they must recognise this from the intonation alone.

5 Ask individual students to read out the tag only for their classmates to identify as A or B.

6 Drill the example sentences from the board.

7 Ask students to give other example sentences with tags and write them on the board. Ask them which intonation pattern the tag should have. Often both are possible, depending on the context. Where this is the case, you could ask students to describe a possible context.

Conducting the game

1 Divide the class into groups of three or four and give each group a board, cards and counters.

2 Explain and/or give out the rules.

3 During the game, move around the class helping students to resolve any disputes. Encourage players to read the sentences and tags to themselves to check that they sound correct before moving their counters.

Intonation monopoly

C

Key

1 have you? (falling)
- You haven't tried very hard,
- You must be hungry. You haven't eaten today,
- You can't go out. You haven't done your homework,
- You can't afford a car. You haven't got any money,

2 have you? (rising)
- You haven't seen my glasses anywhere,
- You haven't taken my keys by mistake,
- You haven't got a pen I could borrow,
- You haven't got a light,

3 can you? (falling)
- You can't write very clearly,
- You can't complain,
- You can't expect to pass if you don't study,
- You can't make an omelette without breaking eggs,

4 can you? (rising)
- You can't remember where I left the keys,
- You can't pass me that book off the shelf,
- You can't remember John's phone number,
- You can't think of a good present for mum,

5 do you? (falling)
- You don't do much to help,
- I'd buy you a beer but you don't drink,
- You're very rude to John. You don't like him,
- There's no sugar, but you don't take sugar in coffee,

6 do you? (rising)
- You don't know where I could buy a stamp around here,
- You don't have an aspirin I could take,
- You don't think I should wear formal clothes,
- You don't think we should take a bottle of wine,

7 is it? (falling)
- It's not very nice weather,
- That dog's not very clever,
- That's not a very good idea,
- This music's not very interesting,

8 is it? (rising)
- The music's not too loud for you,
- How's your headache? It isn't getting worse,
- You live in Hope Street. That's not the one off High Road,
- I hate the name Sue. Your name's not Sue,

9 are they? (falling)
- Those earrings aren't very nice,
- Those flowers aren't very pretty,
- Teachers aren't very well paid,
- These gloves aren't very warm,

10 are they? (rising)
- The shoes I bought you aren't too small for you,
- My dogs aren't annoying you,
- These aren't the keys you're looking for,
- The vegetables aren't too well done,

C9 Intonation monopoly Sheet 1

Rules

1 Place the cards face down in the middle of the board and the counters on the square marked *Start*. Players move around the board. Each time a player passes *Start* he or she may write his or her name on any square on the board; no other player can then land on that square. The first player to pass *Start* three times is the winner.

2 Players take turns to pick up a card and move.

3 When a player picks up a card, he or she must read the sentence on it and complete it with a tag question with the appropriate intonation. If the intonation is correct, the player can then move to the next square with that tag question and that intonation (as marked by the arrow).

4 If a player arrives at a square which is the start of an arrow pointing forwards, he or she can move to the square indicated if he or she can suggest a sentence that would naturally lead to that tag question.

5 If a player arrives at a square which is the start of an arrow pointing backwards, the player must move to the square indicated unless he or she can suggest a sentence that would naturally lead to that tag question.

6 If a player lands on a square with another player's name in it, the player must return to the square he or she came from.

You don't think I should wear formal clothes,	You don't think we should take a bottle of wine,	There's no sugar, but you don't take sugar in coffee,	You don't do much to help,
That dog's not very clever,	This music's not very interesting,	The music's not too loud for you,	It's not very nice weather,
You live in Hope Street. That's not the one off High Road,	The shoes I bought you aren't too small for you,	How's your headache? It isn't getting worse,	That's not a very good idea,
Those flowers aren't very pretty,	These gloves aren't very warm,	These aren't the keys you're looking for,	The vegetables aren't too well done,
My dogs aren't annoying you,	I hate the name Sue. Oh! Your name's not Sue,	Those earrings aren't very nice,	Teachers aren't very well paid,

C9 Intonation monopoly Sheet 3

You must be hungry. You haven't eaten today,	You haven't seen my glasses anywhere,	You haven't taken my keys by mistake,	You haven't tried very hard,
You can't go out. You haven't done your homework,	You can't afford a car. You haven't got any money,	You haven't got a light,	You haven't got a pen I could borrow,
You can't think of a good present for mum,	You can't expect to pass if you don't study,	You can't remember John's phone number,	You can't remember where I left the keys,
You can't make an omelette without breaking eggs,	You can't write very clearly,	You can't complain,	You can't pass me that book off the shelf,
I'd buy you a beer but you don't drink,	You're very rude to John. You don't like him,	You don't know where I could buy a stamp around here,	You don't have an aspirin I could take,

Intonation directions

C

Point: the effect of tonic stress on meaning
Minimum level: intermediate
Game type: a listen and respond game for students working in pairs
Approximate time: 30 minutes

Preparation

Copy the worksheet for each member of the class. The second (more difficult) version consists of two pages.

Presentation

1 Write on the board the following sentence:

Why don't we go to the cinema tonight?

Then write two alternative follow-up sentences on the board:

a I don't want to go to the theatre.
b I can't wait until tomorrow.

2 Read the first sentence with the stress on *tonight.* Ask the class to identify which of the two follow-up sentences they think is implied by the first sentence. (Sentence b is implied.)
3 Invite students to suggest how to say the first sentence to make sentence a the appropriate follow-up sentence. (The stress would have to be on *cinema*.)
4 Drill the two possible ways of saying the first sentence. Notice that for this sentence, there should be falling intonation beginning on the stressed word (either *cinema* or *tonight*). *Wh-* questions tend to have falling intonation.
5 *Yes/no* questions commonly have a rising intonation. To illustrate this, repeat the above procedure with the following sentence:

Do you ever go to rock concerts?

a Or do you just watch them on video?
b Or do you only go to classical concerts?

(Stress *go* for follow-up sentence a and *rock* for follow-up sentence b.)

Conducting the game

1 Give each student a worksheet. Divide the class into pairs (or groups of three if necessary).
2 Explain that one player reads the question, stressing one of the underlined words. The other player must then identify which of the alternatives is implied. Demonstrate the procedure first. Read the questions for students to respond to.
3 If the listener does not give the answer the speaker intended, both players should discuss what went wrong. One point players may disagree on is which stressed word in the question implies which of the alternatives. Move around the class helping students to resolve such disputes or provide the key.

C 10 Intonation directions

Key Game 1

The following are the words that need to be stressed to imply the alternatives:

	left	right
1	plane	your
2	worked	you
3	Joe	Smith
4	me	he
5	cinema	tonight
6	present	birthday
7	you	this
8	rock	go

Follow-up

There is a second, more difficult, version of the game included here. In this version of the game, there are four alternatives to choose from and the listener must respond by saying *North, South, East* or *West.*

Key Game 2

The following are the words that need to be stressed to imply the alternatives:

	North	South	East	West
1	you	do	evening	this
2	Has	finished	Maria	her
3	Are	present	birthday	him
4	hat	black	man	that
5	wine	rabbit	cooked	you
6	new	you	Cathy's	red
7	see	us	you	he
8	rock	you	concerts	go

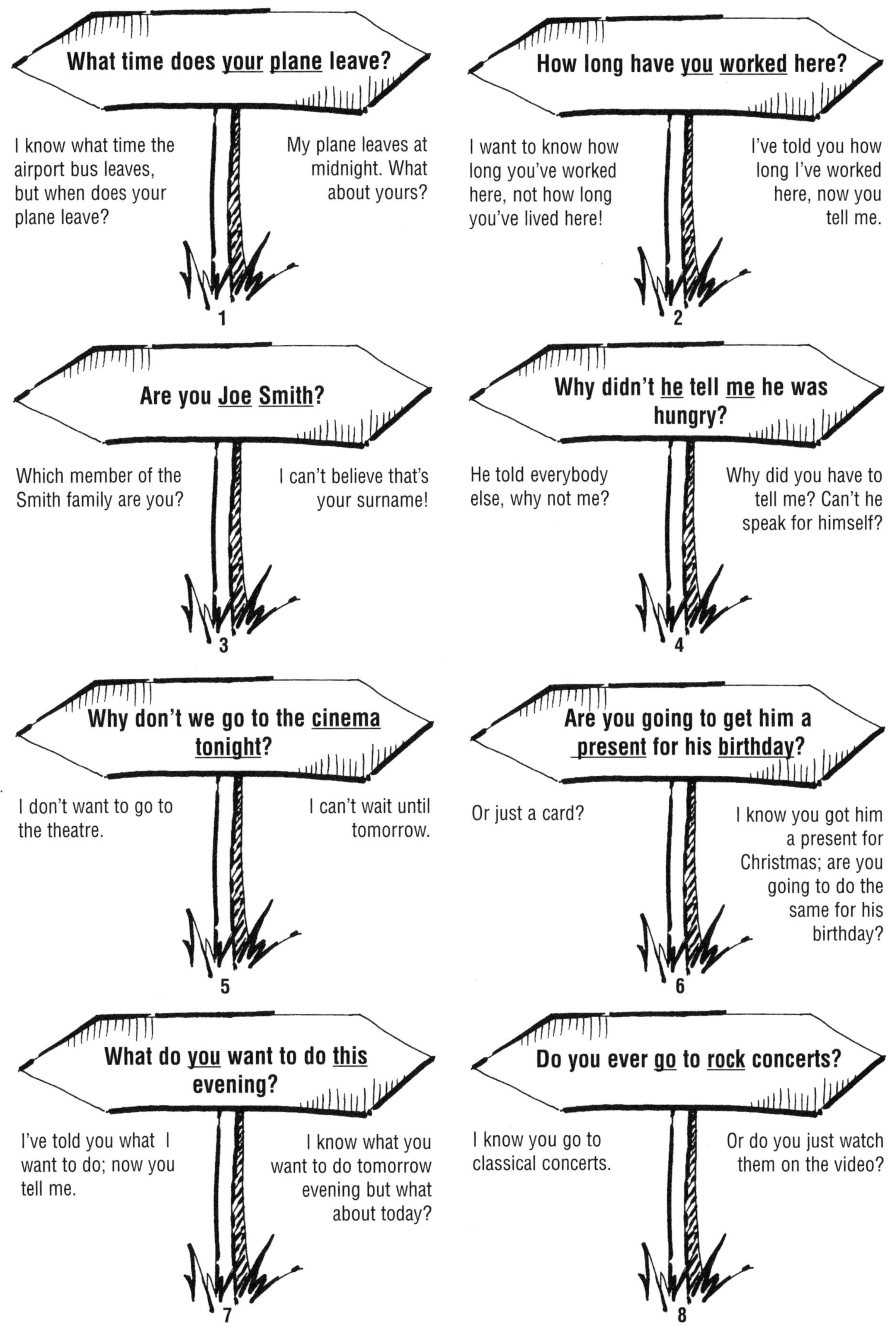
What time does your plane leave?
I know what time the airport bus leaves, but when does your plane leave?
My plane leaves at midnight. What about yours?
1
How long have you worked here?
I want to know how long you've worked here, not how long you've lived here!
I've told you how long I've worked here, now you tell me.
2
Are you Joe Smith?
Which member of the Smith family are you?
I can't believe that's your surname!
3
Why didn't he tell me he was hungry?
He told everybody else, why not me?
Why did you have to tell me? Can't he speak for himself?
4
Why don't we go to the cinema tonight?
I don't want to go to the theatre.
I can't wait until tomorrow.
5
Are you going to get him a present for his birthday?
Or just a card?
I know you got him a present for Christmas; are you going to do the same for his birthday?
6
What do you want to do this evening?
I've told you what I want to do; now you tell me.
I know what you want to do tomorrow evening but what about today?
7
Do you ever go to rock concerts?
I know you go to classical concerts.
Or do you just watch them on the video?
8

C10 Intonation directions Game 2 Sheet 1

N

I've told you what I want to do; now you tell me.

I know what you want to do tomorrow evening, but what about today?

1
What do you want to do this evening?

We've agreed what we want to do this afternoon, but what about this evening?

I know what you don't want to do!

N

Or has she not? Tell me the truth now.

Because if not, she shouldn't be spending so much time helping you with your homework!

2
Has Maria finished her homework yet?

I know Angela's finished, but what about Maria?

Or is she still doing it?

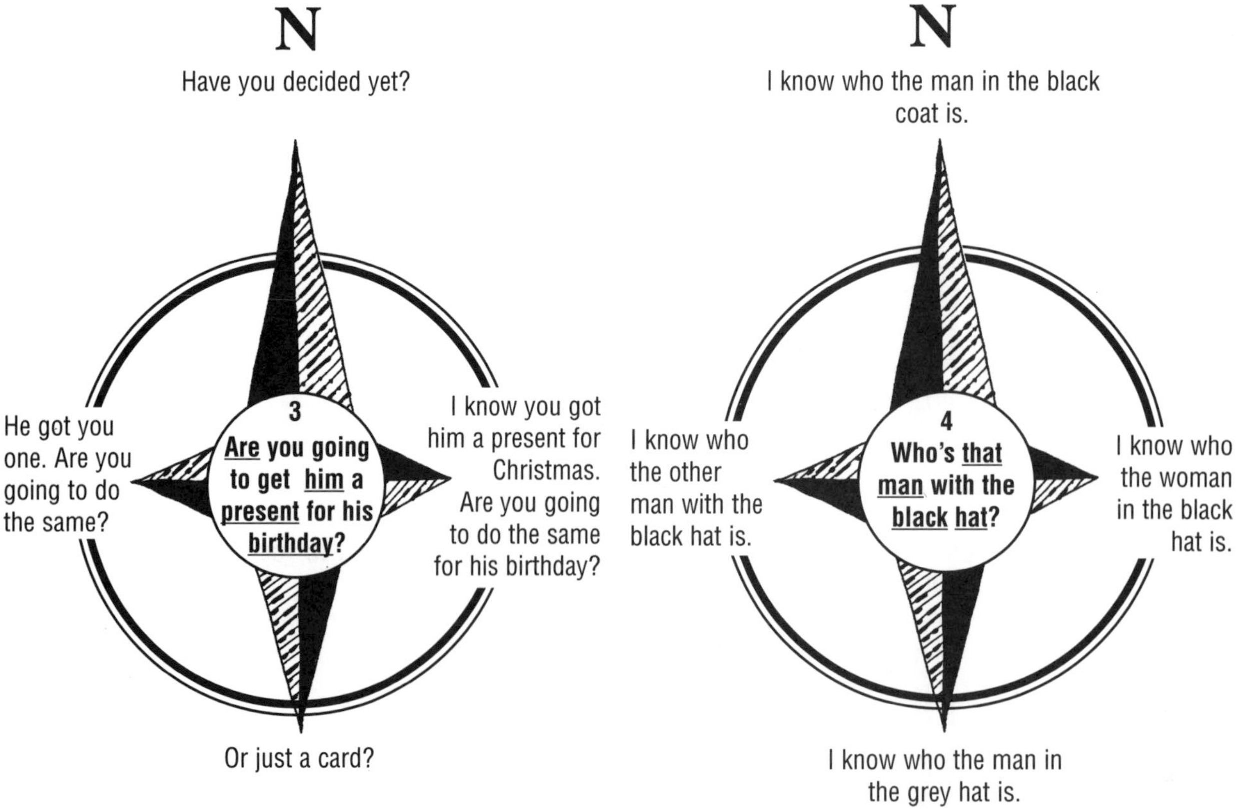

N
Have you decided yet?
He got you one. Are you going to do the same?
3
Are you going to get him a present for his birthday?
I know you got him a present for Christmas. Are you going to do the same for his birthday?
Or just a card?
N
I know who the man in the black coat is.
I know who the other man with the black hat is.
4
Who's that man with the black hat?
I know who the woman in the black hat is.
I know who the man in the grey hat is.

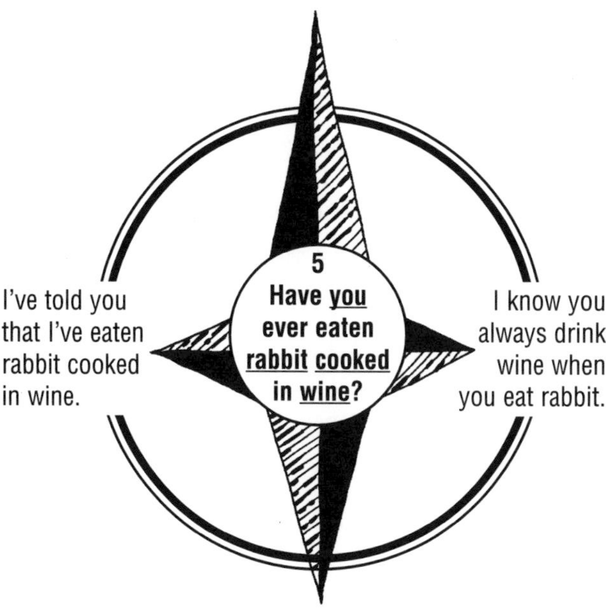
N
I know that you've eaten rabbit cooked in other ways.
I've told you that I've eaten rabbit cooked in wine.
5
Have you ever eaten rabbit cooked in wine?
I know you always drink wine when you eat rabbit.
I know you've eaten chicken in wine.

N
I know you didn't like her old one.
I know what you thought of her new green dress.
6
What did you think of Cathy's new red dress?
I know what you thought of Rita's dress, but what about Cathy's?
I thought it was awful
What about you?

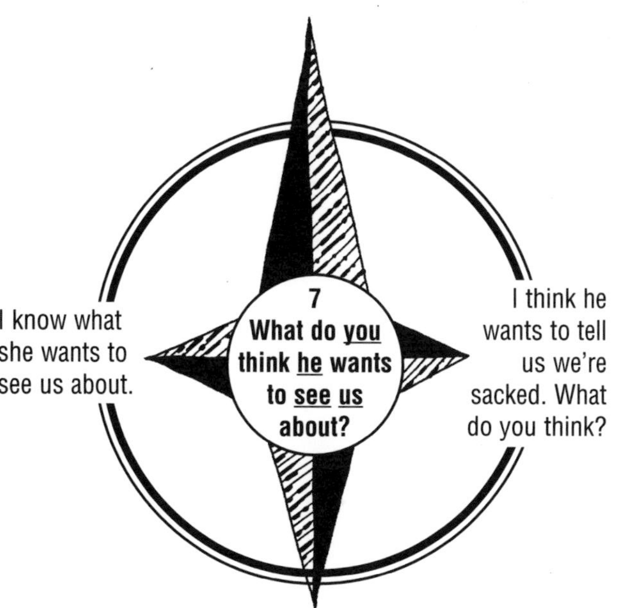
N
Why couldn't he just phone?
I know what she wants to see us about.
7
What do you think he wants to see us about?
I think he wants to tell us we're sacked. What do you think?
And not the other members of staff.

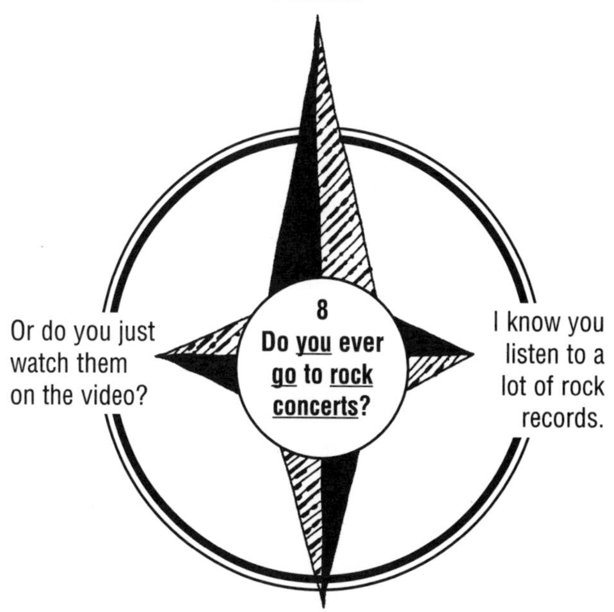
N
I know you go to classical concerts.
Or do you just watch them on the video?
8
Do you ever go to rock concerts?
I know you listen to a lot of rock records.
I often go. What about you?

Acknowledgements

The author would like to thank everybody at the Sociedade Brasileira de Cultura Inglesa in Rio de Janeiro, particularly Rosa Lenzuen and Ralph Bannel, for providing the initial impetus for **Pronunciation Games**, and Lindsay White at CUP for helping to batter it into shape.

Thanks also to Annie McDonald for advice and encouragement given through all stages in the development of the book.

Cover illustration Brent Linley

Book illustrations Mark Hancock

Book design Réalisation

Production Final Film